THE BOOK OF
PIZZAS & PASTA

THE BOOK OF
PIZZAS & PASTA

TED SMART

Specially produced for Ted Smart,
Guardian House, Borough Road,
Godalming, Surrey GU7 2AE.

ISBN 0 85613 035 5

This edition © Salamander Books Ltd. 1991

CREDITS

Designer: Sara Cooper

Contributing authors: Sarah Bush and Lesley Mackley

Typeset by: Maron Graphics Ltd., Wembley

Colour separation by: J. Film Process Ltd., and Kentscan Ltd.

Photographer: Jon Stewart, assisted by Kay Small and Alister Thorpe

Printed in Italy

CONTENTS

PIZZAS

THE HISTORY OF PIZZAS

In Naples one summer, around the late 1800's, Queen Margherita of Savoy was residing with her family in Capodimonte Park. She had heard a lot about pizza and decided to try it for herself. The local pizza maker was summoned and he served her a pizza with a newly invented topping. From then on, the tomato pulp, Mozzarella cheese and fresh basil pizza has been known as Pizza Margherita.

Until this time, pizza had been sold in the streets to people at breakfast, lunch and dinner. It was cut from a large tray that had been cooked in the baker's oven and had a simple topping made of mushrooms and anchovies.

As pizza became more popular, stalls were set up where the dough was shaped as customers ordered. Various toppings were invented including tomato, which had arrived from the New World. This soon developed into the opening of the Pizzeria, an open air place for folk to congregate, eat, drink and discuss. This has gradually become the pizza parlour we have today – which enjoys constant popularity – although the flavour of a pizza made, baked and eaten in the open air is unbeatable.

The dough base of the pizza has been baked in other countries of the Mediterranean for just as long. The French have their own Pissaladière recipe; for the Middle Eastern countries it's pitta bread and Spain uses the dough as a pastry for spicy savoury fillings. Even as far as China the same dough is steamed and served as individual stuffed snacks.

Although enjoying steady and constant popularity, it seems the pizza is now becoming a sophisticated, fashionable food with exotic toppings or turned into unusual shapes, large and small, with exciting fillings. Who knows what will happen to the pizza in years to come!

INGREDIENTS

The traditional pizzas of Italy rely on the wonderful Mediterranean ingredients that are so plentiful – sun-ripened tomatoes, thick olive oil, fresh herbs and cheese are the most well-known, but all sorts of other ingredients can be used as well. There may be some ingredients that you are not familar with.

Olive oil. Indispensable for making a genuine Italian pizza with the authentic flavour.

Olives. Both green and black are used. Olive pulp is made from crushed black olives and is obtainable in jars from Italian food shops and delicatessens.

Capers. These buds from a flowering plant have a delicious, though distinct flavour, so should be used with care.

Oregano (wild marjoram) is used on many pizzas. Use fresh wherever possible.

Thyme can be used fresh or dried.

Parsley, both flat and curly is used.

The small tender sprigs should be chosen and don't consider using the dried type for pizzas, the flavour is not nearly as good.

Basil is quite the best smelling of all the Italian herbs. Use the fresh type whenever possible.

Sweet marjoram is added to pizzas after they are cooked.

Sage should only be used fresh.

Mint should only be used fresh.

Black peppercorns should be used freshly ground as the aroma disappears very quickly, from the ready-ground type.

Nutmeg should be used freshly ground, to obtain the best flavour.

Chillies may be used in fresh form, or use whole dried or crushed type. Remember that chillies vary considerably in size and heat factor, so start with a small amount and gradually increase it.

Dried tomatoes in oil are a wonderful way to preserve tiny tomatoes. These have an unusual, distinct flavour and are available from Italian food shops and delicatessens.

Cheese. Mozzarella, Parmesan, Pecorino, Gorgonzola and Ricotta cheese are all used in traditional pizzas. (Parmesan and Pecorino are at their nicest when freshly grated from a solid piece.)

EQUIPMENT

Flat pizza tin. Metal is essential to conduct the heat and ensure that the base of the pizza is crisp.

Baking sheet. Can be used as an alternative to the flat pizza tin, however, a rim should be formed at the edge of the dough to keep the filling in place.

Rectangular tin or Swiss roll tin. For making the traditional Roman pizza or any that you wish to serve cut in squares.

Deep pan pizza tin. For the thick dough variety of pizza. A sandwich tin or pie tin may be used instead.

Pizza cutter. Makes the job of cutting a pizza far easier than using a knife.

TRADITIONAL PIZZA DOUGH

| 345 g (11 oz/2¾ cups) strong white flour |
| 1 heaped teaspoon salt |
| 15 g (½ oz/3 teaspoons) fresh (compressed) yeast; or 1 teaspoon dried active yeast and 1 teaspoon sugar; or 1 teaspoon easy blend yeast |
| 185 ml (6 fl oz/¾ cup) hand-hot water |
| 1 tablespoon olive oil |

Put flour and salt in a large bowl.

In a small bowl, mix fresh yeast with a little water; put in a warm place until frothy. To use dried active yeast, whisk with sugar and a little water; leave until frothy. Add yeast liquid to flour with remaining water and oil. (To use easy blend yeast, mix into flour and salt before adding water and oil.) Mix to a soft dough; knead on floured surface for 10 minutes. Put in a greased bowl, cover; put in a warm place for 45 minutes or until doubled in size.

Knock back dough and knead briefly. Oil a 30 cm (12 in) pizza tin. Put dough in centre and press out to edges with knuckles. Pinch up edges to create a rim. Use as recipe instructs.

VARIATIONS

If preferred, the dough may be cooked in a 25 x 35.5 cm (10 in x 14 in) Swiss roll tin, or as 4 individual pizzas.

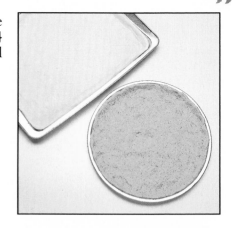

For Herb or Nut Pizza Dough: Knead 2 tablespoons chopped fresh herbs (or 1 tablespoon dried herbs) into the dough. If preferred, knead 30 g (1 oz/¼ cup) chopped walnuts into the dough.

For **Wholemeal Pizza Dough:** Use 315 g (10 oz/2¼ cups) wholemeal flour and 30 g (1 oz/¼ cup) wheatgerm. A little extra water may be required for mixing to form a soft dough.

For **Cornmeal Pizza Dough:** Use 280 g (9 oz/2¼ cups) strong white flour and 60 g (2 oz/⅓ cup) cornmeal.

POTATO PIZZA DOUGH

Sieve potato directly into flour and stir in yeast with remaining water. If using easy blend yeast, add all the hand-hot water at this stage.

1 potato, about 155 g (5 oz) weight
345 g (11 oz/2¾ cups) strong white flour
1 heaped teaspoon salt
15 g (½ oz/3 teaspoons) fresh (compressed) yeast; or 1 teaspoon dried active yeast and 1 teaspoon sugar; or 1 teaspoon easy blend yeast
about 185 ml (6 fl oz/¾ cup) hand-hot water

Scrub the unpeeled potato.

Mix to a soft dough, turn onto a lightly floured surface and knead for 10 minutes until smooth. Place in a clean, lightly oiled bowl and cover with plastic wrap. Put in a warm place for about 45 minutes until dough has doubled in size.

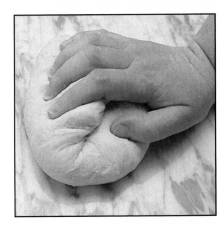

Boil in the skin for 30-40 minutes. Drain and allow to cool sufficiently to remove the skin.

Knock back dough and knead briefly. Oil a 30 cm (12 in) pizza tin. Place dough in the centre and press out to edges with the knuckles. Pinch up edges to create a rim. Use as recipe instructs.

Put flour and salt in a bowl. In a small bowl, cream fresh yeast with a little of the water and put in a warm place until frothy. If using dried active yeast, whisk together with sugar and a little water and set aside. If using easy blend yeast, mix into flour and salt at this stage (do not add any liquid).

Variation: Knead 2 tablespoons chopped fresh herbs or 2 tablespoons freshly grated Parmesan cheese into the dough.

DEEP PAN PIZZA DOUGH

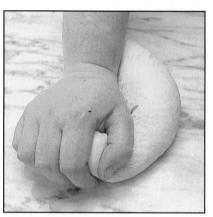

155 g (5 oz/1¼ cups) strong white flour

155 g (5 oz/1¼ cups) plain flour

1 heaped teaspoon salt

15 g (½ oz/3 teaspoons) fresh (compressed) yeast; or 1 teaspoon dried active yeast and 1 teaspoon sugar; or 1 teaspoon easy blend yeast

185 ml (6 fl oz/¾ cup) hand-hot water

1 tablespoon olive oil

Make dough as for Traditional Pizza Dough. When dough has doubled in size, knock back and knead briefly.

Thoroughly oil a 25 cm (10 in) deep pan pizza tin or sandwich tin. Place dough in the centre and press out to edges with the knuckles.

Cover with plastic wrap and put in a warm place for about 1½ hours, until risen almost to the top of tin. Use as recipe instructs.

CRUMBLE PIZZA DOUGH

185 g (6 oz/1½ cups) plain flour

1 teaspoon salt

2 teaspoons caster sugar

60 ml (2 fl oz/¼ cup) vegetable oil

6 teaspoons milk

Sift flour into a large bowl. Stir in salt and sugar. Whisk oil and milk together in measuring jug and pour onto the flour.

Stir with a fork until mixture is crumbly but still moist. It will not form the usual dense dough.

Press mixture onto base and up sides of a 25 cm (10 in) deep pan pizza tin or pie tin. Use as recipe instructs.

SCONE PIZZA DOUGH

PIZZA CARCIOFI

| 125 g (4 oz/1 cup) self-raising wholewheat flour |
| 125 g (4 oz/1 cup) self-raising white flour |
| salt and pepper |
| 60 g (2 oz/¼ cup) butter or margarine |
| about 155 ml (5 fl oz/⅔ cup) milk |

Put flours into a large bowl. Season. Add butter or margarine and rub in with the fingertips until mixture resembles breadcrumbs.

Stir in sufficient milk to form a dough. Turn onto a lightly floured surface and knead briefly.

| 1 quantity Traditional Pizza Dough, shaped and ready for topping, see page 8 |
| TOPPING: |
| 2 tablespoons Tomato Topping, see page 12 |
| 60 g (2 oz/½ cup) grated Fontina cheese |
| 280 g (9 oz) jar artichokes in oil |
| 8 preserved tomatoes in oil |
| salt and pepper |
| parsley, to garnish |

Fontina cheese.

Drain artichokes, reserving the oil. Drain the tomatoes. Slice artichokes and arrange over the cheese. Chop tomatoes roughly and sprinkle over the artichokes. Season to taste with salt and pepper. Sprinkle with 1-2 tablespoons of the reserved artichoke oil.

Bake in the oven for 20 minutes until dough is golden. Serve garnished with parsley.

Serves 4.

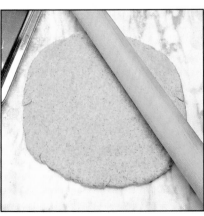

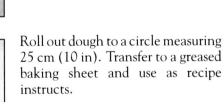

Roll out dough to a circle measuring 25 cm (10 in). Transfer to a greased baking sheet and use as recipe instructs.

Variation: Stir 2 tablespoons chopped fresh parsley into crumb mixture before adding liquid.

Preheat oven to 220C (425F/Gas 7). Spread the dough with Tomato Topping. Sprinkle over the grated

PIZZA NAPOLITANA

1 quantity Traditional Pizza Dough,
shaped and ready for topping, see page 8
TOPPING:
3 tablespoons olive oil
500 g (1 lb) tomatoes
1 clove garlic, crushed
salt and pepper
250 g (8 oz) Mozzarella cheese
50 g (2 oz) can anchovy fillets, drained
1 tablespoon chopped fresh oregano
oregano sprigs, to garnish

Preheat oven to 220C (425F/Gas 7). Brush dough with 1 tablespoon oil. Place tomatoes in a bowl. Pour over boiling water. Leave for 1 minute. Drain, peel and roughly chop. Spread over dough. Sprinkle with garlic and season to taste with salt and pepper.

Slice cheese thinly. Arrange over tomatoes. Chop anchovies and sprinkle over cheese. Sprinkle over oregano and remaining oil. Bake in the oven for 20 minutes until cheese has melted and dough is crisp and golden. Serve the pizza at once, garnished with a few small sprigs of oregano.

Serves 4.

PIZZA MARGHERITA

1 quantity Traditional Pizza Dough,
shaped and ready for topping, see page 8
TOMATO TOPPING:
500 g (1 lb) tomatoes, skinned, see left
or 440 g (14 oz) can chopped tomatoes
2 tablespoons olive oil
1 onion, finely chopped
1 clove garlic, crushed
3 teaspoons tomato purée (paste)
½ teaspoon sugar
3 teaspoons chopped fresh basil
salt and pepper
TO FINISH:
1-2 tablespoons oil
125 g (4 oz) Mozzarella cheese
6-8 fresh basil leaves
basil sprig, to garnish

Make Tomato Topping. Chop tomatoes, if using fresh. Heat oil in saucepan. Add onion and garlic and cook until soft. Stir in tomatoes, tomato purée (paste), sugar and basil and season to taste with salt and pepper. Cover pan and simmer gently for 30 minutes until thick.

Preheat oven to 220C (425F/Gas 7). Brush dough with 1 tablespoon oil. Spoon over tomato topping. Slice Mozzarella thinly. Arrange over sauce. Sprinkle with salt to taste, 2-3 basil leaves and remaining oil. Bake in the oven for 20 minutes until cheese has melted and dough is crisp and golden. Sprinkle with remaining basil leaves. Serve at once, garnished with a sprig of basil.

Serves 4.

PIZZA MARINARA

1 quantity Traditional Pizza Dough,
shaped and ready for topping, see page 8
TOPPING:
3 tablespoons olive oil
250 g (8 oz) tomatoes, skinned, see page
12
3 large cloves garlic, peeled
salt and pepper
few capers, if desired

Preheat oven to 220C (425F/Gas
7). Brush dough with 1 tablespoon
oil. Quarter tomatoes and discard
seeds. Chop roughly and drain in a
sieve. Spread over dough. Cut
garlic into thick slices and sprinkle
over tomatoes.

Season. Sprinkle with oil. Bake
in the oven for 20 minutes until
dough is crisp and golden. Sprinkle
with capers, if desired.

Serves 4.

ROMAN PIZZA

1 quantity Traditional Pizza Dough,
made up to end of step 2, see page 8
TOPPING:
3 tablespoons olive oil
2 large onions, chopped
500 g (1 lb) tomatoes, skinned, see page
12, or 440 g (14 oz) can chopped
tomatoes
185 g (6 oz) can red pimento, drained
50 g (2 oz) can anchovy fillets
12 stoned black olives
pimento and olives, to garnish

Preheat oven to 220C (425F/Gas
7). Lightly grease a 25 x 35.5 cm
(10 x 14 in) Swiss roll tin. Knock
back risen dough and knead briefly.
Place in prepared tin and press out
to edges with knuckles. Pinch up
edges to create a rim.

In a saucepan, heat 2 tablespoons
oil. Cook onions until soft. Chop
tomatoes, if fresh, add to pan and
cook for 2 minutes. Spoon over
dough. Slice pimento in strips and
arrange over tomato. Drain anchovies, cut in half lengthwise and
arrange in a lattice pattern on top.
Halve olives and place in gaps.
Sprinkle with remaining oil.

Bake in the oven for 20 minutes
until dough is crisp and golden.
Garnish with pimento and olives.

Serves 4.

FOUR SEASONS PIZZA

1 quantity Traditional Pizza Dough, made up to end of step 2, see page 8

TOPPING:

3 tablespoons olive oil

60 g (2 oz) button mushrooms

60 g (2 oz) prosciutto (Parma ham)

6 stoned black olives

4 canned artichoke hearts, drained

60 g (2 oz) Mozzarella cheese

1 tomato, skinned, see page 12

salt and pepper

Preheat oven to 220C (425F/Gas 7). Lightly grease a baking sheet. Knock back risen dough and knead briefly. Place dough on baking sheet, press out with knuckles to a circle measuring 25 cm (10 in). Brush dough with a little oil.

Heat 2 tablespoons oil in a saucepan. Cook mushrooms for 5 minutes. Mark dough into 4 equal sections with a knife. Arrange mushrooms over one section. Cut ham in strips and chop olives; place over second section. Slice artichokes thinly. Arrange over third section. Slice cheese and tomato and arrange over fourth section. Season to taste with salt and pepper. Sprinkle with remaining oil. Bake in the oven for 20 minutes until dough is crisp and golden. Serve at once.

Serves 4.

Variation: Make this recipe as 4 individual pizzas, if preferred.

SPICY PORK & PEPPER PIZZA

1 quantity Traditional Pizza Dough, shaped and ready for topping, see page 8

TOPPING:

2 tablespoons olive oil

1 quantity Tomato Topping, see page 12

125 g (4 oz/1 cup) grated Mozzarella cheese

3-4 Italian pork sausages

salt and pepper

1 yellow pepper (capsicum), seeded and chopped

2 tablespoons freshly grated Parmesan cheese

chopped fresh parsley, to garnish

Preheat oven to 220C (425F/Gas 7). Brush dough with 1 tablespoon oil. Spread Tomato Topping over dough. Sprinkle Mozzarella on top. With a sharp knife, cut skins from sausages and discard. Break meat into pieces, scatter over cheese. Season to taste with salt and pepper.

Sprinkle with chopped pepper (capsicum), Parmesan cheese and remaining olive oil. Bake in the oven for 20 minutes until dough is crisp. Garnish with parsley.

Serves 4.

— PROSCIUTTO & OLIVE PIZZA —

1 quantity Traditional Pizza Dough,
shaped and ready for topping, see page 8
TOPPING:
185 g (6 oz) Mozzarella cheese
4 slices prosciutto (Parma ham)
2 tablespoons olive pulp, see Note
2 tablespoons olive oil
salt and pepper
TO GARNISH:
prosciutto (Parma ham)
few olives
basil sprigs

Preheat oven to 220C (425F/Gas
7). Make the topping. Cut cheese
and prosciutto (Parma ham) into
cubes. Place in bowl with olive pulp.
Mix together and moisten with a
little oil if dry. Spread over dough.
Season to taste with salt and pepper
and sprinkle with remaining oil.
Bake in the oven for 20 minutes
until dough is crisp and golden.
Garnish with curls of prosciutto
(Parma ham), olives and basil
sprigs.

Serves 4.

Note: Olive pulp may be bought in
jars from Italian food shops.

— ITALIAN SAUSAGE PIZZA —

1 quantity Traditional Pizza Dough,
shaped and ready for topping, see page 8
TOPPING:
2 tablespoons olive oil
1 quantity Tomato Topping, see page 12
60 g (2 oz) mushrooms, finely sliced
3 spicy Italian sausages or 1 Luganeghe
2 tablespoons freshly grated Pecorino
cheese
salt and pepper
extra grated Pecorino cheese and flat-
leaf parsley, to garnish

Preheat oven to 220C (425F/Gas
7). Brush dough with 1 tablespoon
oil. Spread Tomato Topping over
dough and sprinkle with mushrooms. With a sharp knife, cut skins
from the sausages and discard. Break
meat into pieces and scatter over
mushrooms. Sprinkle with grated
cheese. Season to taste with salt
and pepper.

Sprinkle remaining olive oil over
top. Bake in the oven for 20
minutes until dough is crisp and
golden. Serve garnished with extra
grated Pecorino cheese and flat-leaf
parsley.

Serves 4.

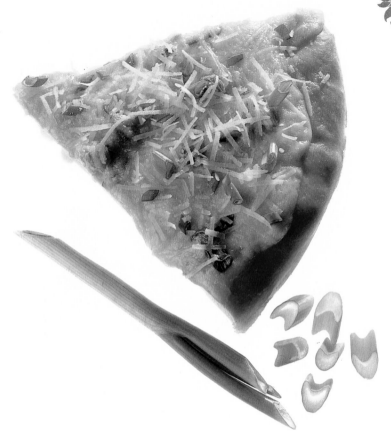

THREE PEPPER PIZZA

1 quantity Traditional Pizza Dough,
shaped and ready for topping, see page 8

TOPPING:

1 red pepper (capsicum)

1 yellow pepper (capsicum)

1 green pepper (capsicum)

2 tomatoes, skinned, see page 12

3 tablespoons olive oil

1 onion, finely chopped

1 clove garlic, crushed

salt and pepper

pinch of dried oregano

oregano sprigs and olives, to garnish

Make the topping. Skin peppers (capsicums): spear one at a time with a fork and hold over a gas flame for 5-10 minutes until black and blistered. Alternatively, halve and seed peppers (capsicums). Place under preheated grill until black. Peel skin off with a knife.

Chop red pepper (capsicum); quarter, seed and chop tomatoes. Put in a saucepan with 2 tablespoons oil, onion and garlic. Cook until soft. Preheat oven to 220C (425F/Gas 7). Brush dough with a little oil.

Spread pepper (capsicum) mixture over dough. Season to taste with salt and pepper. Sprinkle with oregano. Cut remaining peppers (capsicums) in strips. Arrange over pizza. Season to taste with salt and pepper. Sprinkle with remaining oil. Bake in the oven for 20 minutes until dough is crisp and golden. Garnish with oregano and olives.

Serves 4.

FOUR CHEESE PIZZA

1 quantity Traditional Pizza Dough,
shaped and ready for topping, see page 8

TOPPING:

2 tablespoons olive oil

60 g (2 oz) Mozzarella cheese

60 g (2 oz) Gorgonzola cheese

60 g (2 oz) Fontina or Gruyère cheese

60 g (2 oz/½ cup) freshly grated
Parmesan cheese

salt and pepper

chopped spring onion and extra grated
cheese, to garnish

Preheat oven to 220C (425F/Gas 7). Brush dough with 1 tablespoon oil. Cut the 3 cheeses into small cubes. Sprinkle over the dough. Sprinkle over Parmesan, season to taste with salt and pepper. Sprinkle over remaining oil.

Bake in the oven for 20 minutes until cheese is melted and dough is crisp and golden. Garnish with spring onion and extra cheese.

Serves 4.

CRUMPET PIZZAS

4 rashers streaky bacon, rinds removed
8 crumpets
60 g (2 oz/¼ cup) butter
2 tablespoons anchovy paste
4 tomatoes, sliced
8 slices processed Cheddar cheese
4 spring onions
stuffed olives, to garnish

Preheat grill. Grill bacon and crumpets.

Meanwhile, in a bowl, beat butter and anchovy paste together. Spread a little on each crumpet. Arrange tomato slices on top.

Cut cheese slices diagonally into 4 triangular shapes. Arrange on top of crumpets. Grill briefly to melt cheese. Slice spring onions and sprinkle on top. Cut bacon rashers in half crosswise. Roll up and spear on cocktail sticks with stuffed olives. Use to garnish crumpets and serve at once.

Serves 4.

DEVILLED MUFFINS

4 wholemeal muffins
TOPPING:
2 tablespoons vegetable oil
1 tablespoon grated fresh root ginger, if desired
375 g (12 oz) mushrooms, sliced
1 bunch spring onions, sliced
2 teaspoons Worcestershire sauce
½ teaspoon French mustard
salt and pepper
butter for spreading, if desired
spring onion tassels, to garnish

Preheat oven to 200C (400F/Gas 6). Split muffins. Toast under pre-heated grill on both sides.

Meanwhile make topping. Heat oil in a large saucepan. Add ginger, if desired, and fry for 10-15 seconds, stirring.

Add mushrooms; cook stirring for 1 minute. Add spring onions and continue to cook for 10 seconds. Add Worcestershire sauce and mustard and season to taste with salt and pepper. Butter muffins, if desired. Spoon mushroom mixture on top of muffins and bake in the oven for 2-3 minutes. Serve at once, garnished with spring onion tassels.

Serves 4.

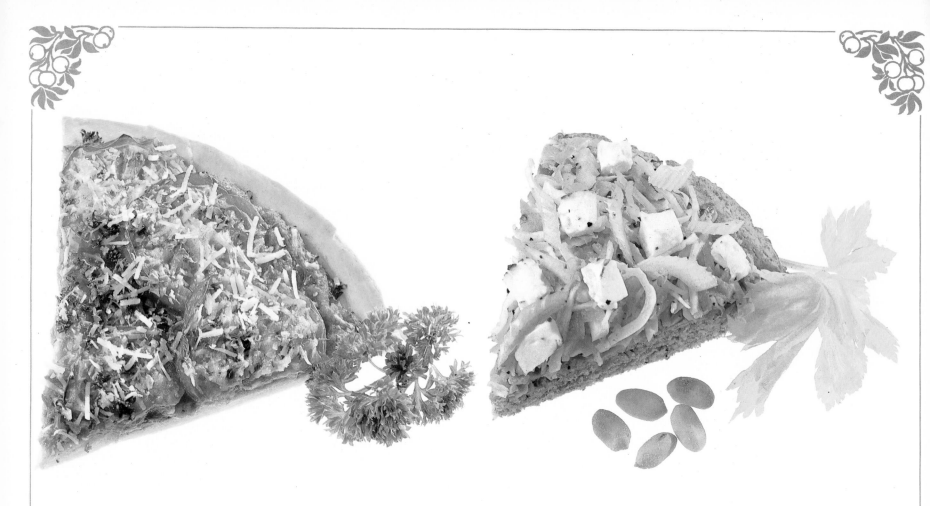

AUBERGINE & TOMATO PIZZA

1 quantity Traditional Pizza Dough, shaped and ready for topping, see page 8

AUBERGINE TOPPING:

500 g (1 lb) aubergines (eggplants)

1 clove garlic, crushed

3 tablespoons lemon juice

3 tablespoons chopped fresh parsley

2 spring onions, chopped

salt and pepper

TO FINISH:

500 g (1 lb) tomatoes, sliced

1 tablespoon olive oil

2 tablespoons chopped fresh parsley

2 tablespoons freshly grated Parmesan cheese

parsley sprigs, to garnish

First make Aubergine Topping. Preheat oven to 180C (350F/Gas 4). Put aubergines (eggplants) on a baking sheet and bake in the oven for 30 minutes until soft. Cool.

Halve and scoop out soft centres into a bowl. Add garlic, lemon juice, parsley and spring onions. Season to taste with salt and pepper.

Increase oven temperature to 220C (425F/Gas 7). Spread aubergine (eggplant) purée over dough. Arrange sliced tomatoes on top, brush with oil and season to taste with salt and pepper. Sprinkle with chopped parsley and Parmesan cheese. Bake in the oven for 20 minutes. Serve garnished with parsley.

Serves 4.

Note: The aubergine purée may be made in advance and refrigerated for 3-4 days. It is also delicious served as a dip with hot toast or pitta bread.

NUTTY VEGETABLE PIZZA

1 quantity Scone Pizza Dough, shaped and ready for topping, see page 11

60 g (2 oz/⅓ cup) roasted peanuts, chopped

TOPPING:

¼ small white cabbage

2 carrots

2 sticks celery

2 tablespoons French dressing

salt and pepper

125 g (4 oz) full fat soft cheese, cubed

peanuts and celery leaves, to garnish

Preheat oven to 220C (425F/Gas 7). Cover dough with the chopped peanuts and press in lightly. Bake in the oven for 15 minutes.

Meanwhile, shred cabbage, grate carrots and slice celery thinly. Place vegetables in a bowl. Add the French dressing and season to taste with salt and pepper.

Spoon vegetables over the pizza. Arrange cubes of cheese on top. Return to oven and bake for a further 10 minutes. Serve at once, sprinkled with peanuts and garnished with celery leaves.

Serves 4.

— PESTO & MUSHROOM PIZZA —

1 quantity Deep Pan Pizza Dough, shaped and ready for topping, see page 10

PESTO TOPPING:

1 large bunch fresh basil leaves

3 cloves garlic, peeled

60 g (2 oz/⅓ cup) pine nuts

3 tablespoons freshly grated Parmesan cheese

salt and pepper

155 ml (5 fl oz/⅔ cup) olive oil

a little boiling water

TO FINISH:

185 g (6 oz) button mushrooms, sliced

a little olive oil

90 g (3 oz/⅔ cup) grated Mozzarella cheese

90 g (3 oz/⅔ cup) freshly grated Parmesan cheese

basil sprigs and pine nuts, to garnish

Preheat oven to 220C (425F/Gas 7). Make topping. In a blender or food processor, put basil leaves, garlic, pine nuts and Parmesan cheese and season to taste with salt and pepper. Switch on machine and pour in oil in a gentle stream until absorbed. Blend until smooth, adding a little boiling water if necessary, to achieve a spreading consistency.

Spread topping over dough. Arrange mushrooms on top; brush with olive oil. Sprinkle with Mozzarella cheese and Parmesan cheese. Bake in the oven for 20 minutes until dough is well risen and golden. Serve garnished with basil and pine nuts.

Serves 4.

Note: Pesto can be made in advance and stored in a screw-topped jar in the refrigerator for up to 6 days. Ready-made pesto may be bought from delicatessen counters in supermarkets and from specialist food shops.

— TAPENADE & PEPPER PIZZA —

1 quantity Deep Pan Pizza Dough, shaped and ready for topping, see page 10

TAPENADE TOPPING:

155 g (5 oz) stoned green olives

60 g (2 oz) can anchovy fillets

60 g (2 oz) canned tuna fish in oil, drained

30 g (1 oz) capers

1 clove garlic

1 teaspoon Dijon mustard

a little olive oil

salt and pepper

a little lemon juice

TO FINISH:

1 green pepper (capsicum), skinned, see page 16

1 yellow pepper (capsicum), skinned

mint sprigs and a few capers, to garnish

Preheat oven to 220C (425F/Gas 7). Make the topping. In a blender or food processor, put the olives, anchovy fillets and oil, tuna fish, capers, garlic and mustard. Blend to a rough-textured purée. Add a little extra oil if necessary. Season with salt and pepper and lemon juice.

Cut skinned peppers (capsicums) into strips and then into diamond shapes. Spread tapenade over dough. Arrange peppers attractively on top. Trickle a little more oil over and season with pepper. Bake in the oven for 20 minutes until dough is golden and well risen. Serve garnished with mint sprigs and capers.

Serves 4.

FRENCH BREAD PIZZA

1 medium French stick
4 tablespoons olive oil
440 g (14 oz) can tomatoes
salt and pepper
220 g (7 oz) can tuna fish in oil, drained
6-8 pimento-stuffed olives
60 g (2 oz/½ cup) grated Edam cheese
3 spring onions, chopped
TO SERVE:
green salad

Preheat oven to 180C (350F/Gas 4). Cut a slice from the top of French stick along whole length. Scoop out most of the soft crumb from base portion (this and the lid will not be required but can be used for breadcrumbs).

Brush inside of loaf with half the olive oil. Drain tomatoes and reserve juice. Brush inside of loaf with juice. Place loaf on a baking sheet and bake in the oven for 10 minutes.

Chop tomatoes and arrange half inside the loaf. Season to taste with salt and pepper. Flake tuna fish and spoon over tomatoes. Season again. Top with remaining tomatoes and season once again.

Halve olives and arrange on top. Sprinkle with grated cheese. Return to oven and bake for a further 15 minutes. Sprinkle with chopped spring onions and serve at once with salad.

Serves 2.

CHEESE & ONION PIZZAS

8 small pitta breads
CHEESE TOPPING:
30 g (1 oz/6 teaspoons) butter or margarine
15 g (½ oz/6 teaspoons) plain flour
250 g (8 oz/2 cups) grated Cheddar cheese
75 ml (2½ fl oz/⅓ cup) milk
1 egg yolk
pinch of dry mustard
pinch of cayenne pepper
TO FINISH:
3 spring onions, chopped
2 eggs, hard-boiled and chopped
hard-boiled egg and chives, to garnish

Preheat oven to 220C (425F/Gas 7). Make the topping. In a saucepan, melt butter or magarine. Add flour and cook, stirring, until smooth. Stir in half the grated cheese, then half the milk. Repeat with remaining cheese and milk. Beat in egg yolk. Stir in mustard and cayenne pepper and mix well.

Place pitta breads on a greased baking sheet. Spread topping over them. Bake in the oven for 10 minutes. In a bowl, mix chopped spring onions and hard-boiled eggs together. Sprinkle the mixture over the pizzas and cook for a further 2 minutes. Serve at once, garnished with slices of hard-boiled egg and chives.

Serves 4.

CREAMY SALMON PIZZA

1 quantity Wholemeal Pizza Dough, shaped and ready for topping, see page 8
1 tablespoon olive oil
TOPPING:
439 g (15½ oz) can red salmon
1 courgette (zucchini), finely chopped
3 tablespoons double (thick) cream
salt and pepper
1 teaspoon grated lemon peel
1 tablespoon chopped fresh dill
30 g (1 oz/¼ cup) grated Parmesan cheese
lemon peel and dill sprigs, to garnish

Preheat oven to 220C (425F/Gas 7). Make the topping. Drain salmon and remove bones. Put in a bowl and flake with a fork. Stir in courgette (zucchini), cream, salt and pepper, lemon peel and dill.

Brush dough with olive oil. Spoon the salmon mixture on top. Sprinkle with the Parmesan cheese. Bake in the oven for 20 minutes until the dough is golden. Serve garnished with lemon and dill.

Serves 4.

CHEESY SEAFOOD PIZZA

1 quantity Traditional Pizza Dough, shaped and ready for topping, see page 8
TOPPING:
1 quantity Cheese Topping, see page 20
220 g (7 oz) can tuna fish in brine
185 g (6 oz) peeled prawns, thawed if frozen
¼ teaspoon paprika
salt and pepper
lemon twists, coriander sprigs and peeled prawns, to garnish, if desired

Preheat oven to 220C (425F/Gas 7). Spread the Cheese Topping over the pizza dough.

Drain tuna fish, put in a bowl and flake roughly with a fork. Mix in prawns and paprika and season to taste with salt and pepper. Spread mixture evenly over the Cheese Topping.

Bake in the oven for 20 minutes until the dough is crisp and golden. Serve the pizza at once, garnished with lemon twists, sprigs of coriander and peeled prawns, if desired.

Serves 4.

FRITTATA PIZZA

1 quantity Traditional Pizza Dough,
made up to end of step 2, see page 8

TOPPING:

2 tablespoons olive oil

1 onion, thinly sliced

3 new potatoes, cooked and sliced

8 slices pepper salami, rind removed

1 small green pepper (capsicum), sliced

8 stoned black olives, halved

60 g (2 oz/⅓ cup) full fat soft cheese,
cubed

1 tablespoon chopped fresh parsley

4 cherry tomatoes, halved

6 eggs

salt and pepper

watercress, to garnish

Preheat oven to 220C (425F/Gas
7). Grease a 25 cm (10 in) deep pan

pizza tin or sandwich tin. Knock
back risen dough and knead briefly,
then press dough into tin.

Brush dough with a little of the
oil. Arrange sliced onion over the
top. Sprinkle with remaining oil.
Bake in the oven for 10 minutes.

Remove pizza from oven. Arrange sliced potatoes, salami, pepper (capsicum), olives and cheese
over the surface. Add parsley and
tomatoes. In a bowl, beat together
eggs and season to taste with salt
and pepper. Pour over pizza and bake
for 10-15 minutes until topping is
puffed and golden. Serve garnished
with watercress.

Serves 4.

AVOCADO & CRAB BITES

1 quantity Traditional Pizza Dough,
made up to end of step 2, see page 8

TOPPING:

2 ripe avocados

1 tablespoon lemon juice

30 g (1 oz/6 teaspoons) butter

30 g (1 oz/¼ cup) plain flour

315 ml (10 fl oz/1¼ cups) milk

salt and pepper

¼ teaspoon cayenne pepper

375 g (12 oz) crabmeat, thawed if frozen
and drained

60 g (2 oz/½ cup) grated Gruyère
cheese

avocado slices and tomato, to garnish

Preheat oven to 220C (425F/Gas
7). Knock back risen dough and
knead briefly. Roll out dough and
use to line a Swiss roll tin.

Make topping. Halve avocados,
remove stones. Scoop out flesh and
chop roughly. Place in a bowl with
lemon juice and stir lightly to coat.
Set aside.

Melt butter in a saucepan. Stir in
flour and cook for 2 minutes. Stir in
milk, bring to the boil and simmer
for 2 minutes. Season to taste with
salt and pepper and cayenne.

Remove pan from heat. Stir in
crab, cheese and avocado. Spread
over the dough, then bake in the
oven for 20 minutes until dough is
golden. Cool slightly before cutting
into fingers or squares. Serve garnished with avocado and tomato.

Serves 6-8.

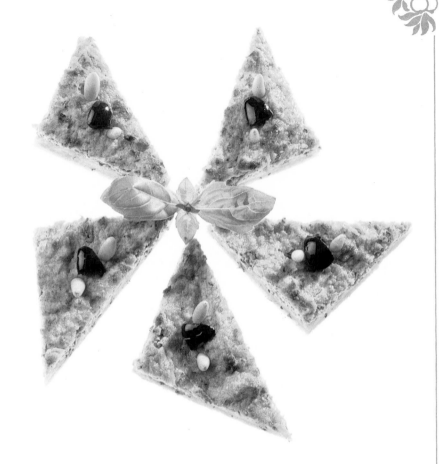

HAM & TOMATO BITES

1 quantity Traditional Pizza Dough,
made to end of step 2, see page 8

TOPPING:

1 quantity Tomato Topping, see page 12

12-14 slices coppa, or Parma, smoked ham

185 g (6 oz) Mozzarella cheese, sliced

olives, anchovies and thyme sprigs, to
garnish

Preheat oven to 220C (425F/Gas
7). Grease several baking sheets.
Roll out dough very thinly and cut
out 12-14 circles with a 4-5 cm
(1½-2 in) cutter.

Spread dough with Tomato Topping. Top each circle with a slice of
coppa, or Parma, ham and a slice of
Mozzarella. Bake in the oven for
10-15 minutes until the dough is
cooked and the cheese has melted.
Serve at once, garnished with
olives, anchovies and thyme.

Serves 6-8.

PESTO PIZZELLE

1 quantity Traditional Pizza Dough,
made to end of step 2, see page 8

TOPPING:

185 g (6 oz) ricotta cheese

3 tablespoons Pesto Topping, see page 19

1 egg, beaten

basil sprigs, black olives and pine nuts,
to garnish

Preheat oven to 220C (425F/Gas
7). Knock back risen dough and
knead briefly. Roll out dough and
use to line a Swiss roll tin.

Make the topping. Beat together
ricotta cheese and sufficient Pesto
Topping and egg to make a smooth,
firm mixture.

Spread over the dough, then
bake in the oven for 20 minutes
until the dough is golden. Cool
slightly, then cut into squares or
triangles. Garnish with basil, olives
and pine nuts. Serve as a cocktail
snack.

Serves 10-20.

FRESH HERB PIZZA

1 quantity Scone Pizza Dough, shaped and ready for topping, see page 11
TOPPING:
2 tablespoons olive oil
1 tablespoon chopped fresh basil
1 tablespoon chopped fresh parsley
1 teaspoon chopped fresh oregano
185 g (6 oz/1 ½ cups) grated Mozzarella cheese
90 g (3 oz/¾ cup) grated Pecorino cheese
salt and pepper
fresh herbs, to garnish

Preheat oven to 220C (425F/Gas 7). Brush the dough with 1 tablespoon oil. Sprinkle with chopped herbs. Cover with the cheeses and season to taste with salt and pepper. Drizzle over the remaining oil. Bake in the oven to 20 minutes until golden. Serve garnished with herbs.

Serves 4.

ASPARAGUS HAM SQUARES

1 quantity Traditional Pizza Dough, made up to end of step 2, see page 8
1 tablespoon vegetable oil
TOPPING:
185 g (6 oz) sliced ham
185 g (6 oz) curd cheese
2 tablespoons single (light) cream or milk
250 g (8 oz) asparagus spears, cooked
salt and pepper
freshly grated Parmesan cheese

Preheat oven to 220 C (425F/Gas 7). Grease a 25 x 35.5 cm (10 x 14 in) Swiss roll tin. Knock back risen dough and knead briefly. Roll out dough on a lightly floured surface and use to line base and sides of tin. Prick base with a fork. Brush with oil. Bake in the oven for 15 minutes until crisp and golden.

Meanwhile, finely chop 125 g (4 oz) ham. Put in a bowl with the cheese and cream or milk. Cut tips from asparagus and reserve. Chop stalks and stir into cheese mixture.

Remove pizza from oven and allow to cool slightly. Spread cheese mixture over dough. Slice remaining ham in strips and arrange in a lattice pattern over dough. Dot asparagus tips on surface, season to taste with salt and pepper and sprinkle with Parmesan cheese. Return to oven and cook for a further 2 minutes. Slide pizza from tin onto a chopping board. With a sharp knife cut off crusts and discard. Cut pizza into small squares or fingers (or other shapes, if preferred) and serve as a cocktail snack.

Serves 8-10.

RATATOUILLE & PRAWN PIZZA

1 quantity Wholemeal Pizza Dough,
shaped and ready for topping, see page 8

1 tablespoon vegetable oil

TOPPING:

2 tablespoons vegetable oil

1 large onion, chopped

2 cloves garlic, crushed

3 small courgettes (zucchini), halved

1 small red pepper (capsicum), seeded

1 small green pepper (capsicum), seeded

1 small yellow pepper (capsicum), seeded

250 g (8 oz) aubergine (eggplant), cubed

440 g (14 oz) can chopped tomatoes

2 tablespoons tomato purée (paste)

salt and pepper

125 g (4 oz) peeled prawns, thawed if
frozen

chopped parsley, to garnish

Make the topping. Heat oil in a
large saucepan. Add onion and
garlic. Cook for 3 minutes, stirring
and taking care not to let garlic
burn.

Cut courgettes (zucchini) and
peppers (capsicums) into 1 cm (½
in) pieces. Add to pan with aubergine (eggplant). Add tomatoes,
tomato purée (paste) and season to
taste with salt and pepper. Stir well
and cook for 15 minutes until vegetables are cooked and the sauce
thickened.

Preheat oven to 220C (425F/Gas
7). Prick dough with a fork and
brush with oil. Bake in the oven for
15 minutes. Stir prawns into vegetables and spoon on top of dough.
Bake for a further 5 minutes. Serve
at once sprinkled with chopped
parsley.

Serves 4.

MIXED SEAFOOD PIZZA

1 quantity Traditional Pizza Dough,
shaped and ready for topping, see page 8

TOPPING:

250 g (8 oz) mussels in the shell

2 tablespoons olive oil

2 cloves garlic, crushed

125 g (4 oz) squid, cleaned

440 g (14 oz) can chopped tomatoes

salt and pepper

125 g (4 oz) raw Mediterranean (king)
prawns, thawed if frozen

250 g (8 oz) clean shelled clams or 144 g
(14 oz) canned clams in brine, drained

2 tablespoons chopped fresh parsley

flat-leaf parsley and lemon, to garnish

Make topping. Scrub mussels and
remove beards. Place in a large
saucepan with 2 tablespoons water.
Cover and cook over moderate heat,
shaking pan, until all the shells are
open.

Strain pan juices and reserve. In
a saucepan, heat 1 tablespoon oil
and garlic. Slice squid and add to
pan. Cook for 5 minutes, stirring.
Remove with a slotted spoon and
reserve. Discard garlic. Add tomatoes, reserved mussel juice and
season to taste with salt and pepper.
Cook gently for 30 minutes.

Preheat oven to 220C (425F/Gas
7). Brush dough with remaining oil;
prick with a fork. Bake in the oven
for 15-20 minutes until golden.
Peel prawns; add to sauce with the
clams. Cook for 10 minutes. Stir in
squid and mussels. Remove pizza
from oven. Spoon over fish and
sauce, sprinkle with chopped
parsley and return to oven for 10
minutes. Garnish with parsley and
lemon and serve at once.

Serves 4.

PIZZA CANAPÉS

1 quantity Cornmeal Pizza Dough, made up to end of step 2, see page 8

TOPPING:

1 quantity Cheese Topping, see page 20
a selection of the following: anchovy fillets, stuffed and plain; olives; capers; lumpfish roe; cooked prawns; smoked salmon; crispy bacon; smoked quails' eggs; sprigs of fresh herbs

Preheat oven to 220C (425F/Gas 7). Grease several baking sheets. Knock back risen dough and knead briefly. Roll out dough very thinly and cut out 10-12 small circles with a 4-5 cm (1½-2 in) cutter (or cut into fingers, if preferred). Spread with a little Cheese Topping and arrange on baking sheets. Bake in the oven for 15-20 minutes until golden. Top with any selection of toppings and serve at once.

Serves 10-12.

MOZZOLIVE BITES

1 quantity Cornmeal Pizza Dough, made up to end of step 2, see page 8

TOPPING:

4 tablespoons olive oil
185 g (6 oz) Mozzarella cheese
170 g (5½ oz) jar olive paste
salt and pepper
sage leaves and pimento, to garnish

Preheat oven to 220C (425F/Gas 7). Grease several baking sheets. Knock back risen dough and knead briefly. Roll out dough and cut as for Pizza Canapés, see left. Brush with 1 tablespoon oil and bake in the oven for 15-20 minutes until golden.

Cut Mozzarella into tiny pieces and place in a bowl. Stir in the olive paste. Season to taste with salt and pepper. Spoon a little of the mixture onto each circle, dividing it equally between them.

Sprinkle with a little oil. Bake for a further 3-4 minutes until cheese melts. Garnish with sage leaves and pimento. Serve at once as a cocktail snack.

Serves 10-12.

ARTICHOKE & EMMENTAL PIZZA

1 quantity Traditional Pizza Dough, shaped and ready for topping, see page 8

TOPPING:

3 tablespoons olive oil

440 g (14 oz) can artichoke hearts

salt and pepper

250 g (8 oz/2 cups) grated Emmental cheese

marjoram leaves and sliced pimento, to garnish

Preheat oven to 220C (425F/Gas 7). Brush the pizza dough with 1 tablespoon of the olive oil.

Drain artichokes and slice thinly. Arrange artichoke slices over dough. Sprinkle with remaining oil; season to taste with salt and pepper. Sprinkle the grated Emmental cheese over the top.

Bake in the oven for 20 minutes until dough is crisp and golden and cheese has melted. Serve at once, garnished with marjoram leaves and sliced pimento.

Serves 4.

THREE SALAMI PIZZA

1 quantity Scone Pizza Dough, shaped and ready for topping, see page 11

1 tablespoon vegetable oil

TOPPING:

3 tomatoes, finely chopped

salt and pepper

125 g (4 oz) mixed sliced salami, rinds removed

60 g (2 oz/½ cup) grated Cheddar cheese

gherkins, to garnish

Preheat oven to 220C (425F/Gas 7). Brush dough with the oil.

Spread tomatoes over surface. Season to taste with salt and pepper. Cut salami into strips and arrange over tomatoes. Sprinkle with grated cheese. Bake in the oven for 20 minutes until dough is golden and cheese melted. Serve garnished with gherkins.

Serves 4.

MUSHROOM & CHEESE PIZZA

1 quantity Wholemeal Pizza Dough,
shaped and ready for topping, see page 8

TOPPING:

1-2 tablespoons French mustard or 30 g
(1 oz/6 teaspoons) butter or margarine,
melted

125 g (4 oz) sliced ham

125 g (4 oz) mushrooms, sliced

6 tablespoons crushed, sieved tomatoes

125 g (4 oz/1 cup) grated Cheddar cheese

salt and pepper

watercress sprigs, to garnish

Preheat oven to 220C (425F/Gas
7). Spread dough with the French
mustard, if using, or brush with the
melted butter or margarine.

Slice the ham diagonally to form
diamond shapes. Arrange over
dough. Place one-third of the
mushrooms in the centre and the
remainder in groups around the
edge of the pizza. Spoon a little
tomato over mushrooms. Sprinkle
with grated cheese. Season to taste
with salt and pepper and bake in the
oven for 20 minutes until dough is
crisp and golden and the cheese
bubbling. Garnish with watercress.

Serves 6.

BLT PIZZA

1 quantity Traditional Pizza Dough,
shaped and ready for topping, see page 8

FILLING:

8 streaky bacon rashers, rinds removed

½ small iceberg lettuce

4 tomatoes, roughly chopped

4-6 tablespoons mayonnaise

salt and pepper

shredded lettuce, to garnish

Preheat oven to 200C (400F/Gas
6). Grill bacon until cooked. Drain
on absorbent kitchen paper, then
with kitchen scissors, cut into
pieces. Very finely shred the lettuce.
In a bowl, mix bacon, tomatoes,
lettuce and mayonnaise and season
to taste with salt and pepper.

Spread the mixture over the
dough. Bake in the oven for 20
minutes until the dough is crisp and
golden. Serve at once, garnished
with shredded lettuce.

Serves 4.

MINCE & PICKLE PIZZA

1 quantity Potato Pizza Dough, shaped and ready for topping, see page 9

TOPPING:

250 g (8 oz) ground beef

salt and pepper

2 tablespoons tomato purée (paste)

2 tablespoons Worcestershire sauce

3 tablespoons vegetable oil

4 tablespoons sweet pickle

125 g (4 oz) mushrooms, sliced

1 green pepper (capsicum), sliced

1 small onion, sliced

watercress, chives and red pepper (capsicum), to garnish

Make the topping. In a saucepan, cook the beef until browned. Season to taste with salt and pepper. Add tomato purée (paste) and Worcestershire sauce. Cook for 15 minutes, stirring the mixture occasionally.

Preheat oven to 220C (425F/Gas 7). Brush dough with 1 tablespoon oil. Spread pickle over the dough. Arrange mushrooms on top. Spoon meat mixture on top. Arrange rings of pepper (capsicum) and onion over and brush with remaining oil. Bake in the oven for 20 minutes until dough is crisp and golden. Serve garnished with watercress bunches tied with chives and red pepper (capsicum).

Serves 4.

SARDINE & TOMATO PIZZA

1 quantity Traditional Pizza Dough, shaped and ready for topping, see page 8

TOPPING:

4 tablespoons tomato ketchup (sauce)

125 g (4 oz) can sardines in oil, drained

2 tomatoes, sliced

4 processed cheese slices

mustard and cress, to garnish

Preheat oven to 220C (425F/Gas 7). Spread tomato ketchup (sauce) over the dough. Split sardines horizontally and arrange around the edge. Make a circle of overlapping tomatoes in the centre.

Cut cheese in strips and arrange in a lattice over the tomatoes. Bake in the oven for 20 minutes until the dough is golden. Serve at once, garnished with mustard and cress.

Serves 6.

BOLOGNESE PIZZA

1 quantity Potato Pizza Dough, with Parmesan cheese, shaped and ready for topping, see page 9

TOPPING:

2 tablespoons vegetable oil

60 g (2 oz) rashers streaky bacon, chopped

1 onion, finely chopped

1 carrot, finely chopped

1 stick celery, finely chopped

1 clove garlic, crushed

250 g (8 oz) ground beef

1 tablespoon tomato purée (paste)

pinch of mixed herbs

125 ml (4 fl oz/½ cup) beef stock

salt and pepper

TO SERVE:

freshly grated Parmesan cheese

tomato and marjoram sprigs, to garnish

Make the topping. In a saucepan, heat oil and cook the bacon for 2 minutes. Add onion, carrot, celery and garlic. Cook, stirring, until soft. Add ground beef and cook, stirring until brown.

Stir in tomato purée (paste), herbs and stock and season to taste with salt and pepper. Cover and cook gently for 30 minutes.

Preheat oven to 220C (425F/Gas 7). Spoon sauce on top of dough and spread over. Bake in the oven for 20 minutes until dough is crisp and golden. Serve sprinkled with Parmesan cheese and garnished with tomato and marjoram.

Serves 6.

TUNA & ONION PIZZA

1 quantity Deep Pan Pizza Dough, shaped and ready for topping, see page 10

TOPPING:

2 tablespoons vegetable oil

440 g (14 oz) can chopped tomatoes

1 bunch spring onions, chopped

220 g (7 oz) can tuna fish, drained

salt and pepper

Preheat oven to 220C (425F/Gas 7). Brush dough with 1 tablespoon oil. Bake in the oven for 20 minutes until golden and well risen.

Make the topping. In a saucepan, heat the tomatoes and remaining oil. Add half the spring onions to pan and cook for 10 minutes. Flake tuna fish roughly, stir into tomato mixture. Season to taste with salt and pepper.

Spoon onto dough and bake in the oven for 3-5 minutes. Shred remaining chopped spring onions and sprinkle over pizza to serve.

Serves 6.

FRENCH BRIE PIZZA

1 quantity Traditional Pizza Dough, with walnuts, shaped and ready for topping, see page 8

TOPPING:

2 small leeks, finely shredded

2 tablespoons walnut or olive oil

salt

250 g (8 oz) Brie or Camembert cheese

1 teaspoon green peppercorns in brine, drained

15 g (½ oz/2 tablespoons) chopped walnuts

Preheat oven to 220C (425F/Gas 7). Make the topping. Put leeks in a saucepan with 1 tablespoon oil. Cook gently for 5 minutes, stirring until soft. Brush dough with remaining oil, then spoon over the leeks. Season to taste with salt.

Slice cheese thinly, arrange over leeks. Lightly crush some or all of the peppercorns and sprinkle over leeks. Scatter walnuts over top. Bake in the oven for 20 minutes until dough is crisp and golden.

Serves 4.

PIZZA WITH CLAMS

1 quantity Wholemeal Pizza Dough, shaped and ready for topping, see page 8

TOPPING:

500 g (1 lb) clams in the shell or 440 g (14 oz) can clams in juice

3 tablespoons olive oil

1 quantity Tomato Topping, see page 12

salt and pepper

few drops chilli sauce

2 tablespoons chopped fresh parsley

Preheat oven to 220C (425F/Gas 7). If using clams in the shell, wash well and place in a saucepan with 1 tablespoon oil. Cover and cook over gentle heat until all the shells open. Remove from heat; strain pan juices into a bowl. Reserve. Remove clams from their shells, reserving a few intact for garnishing. Place shelled clams in reserved juice.

Spread Tomato Topping over pizza dough. Sprinkle with remaining oil. Season to taste with salt and pepper, a sprinkling of chilli sauce and 1 tablespoon chopped parsley. Bake in the oven for 15 minutes. Spoon the shelled clams (or canned clams) and a little clam juice over pizza; cook for a further 5 minutes. Arrange reserved clams in shells on top. Sprinkle the pizza with remaining chopped parsley and serve at once.

Serves 4.

MEXICAN CHILLI PIZZA

1 quantity Cornmeal Pizza Dough, made up to end of step 2, see page 8

TOPPING:

500 g (1 lb) minced beef

1 onion, chopped

1 clove garlic, crushed

salt and pepper

1 teaspoon ground cumin

1 teaspoon chilli powder

2 teaspoons tomato purée (paste)

432 g (15.25 oz) can kidney beans, drained

3 tomatoes, chopped

220 g (7 oz) can sweetcorn, drained

1 green pepper (capsicum), chopped

4-6 spring onions, chopped

60 g (2 oz/½ cup) grated Cheddar cheese

GUACAMOLE:

2 ripe avocados

juice of 1 lemon

salt and pepper

3 spring onions

few drops Tabasco sauce

Preheat oven to 220C (425F/Gas 7). Grease a 23 x 35.5 cm (10 x 14 in) Swiss roll tin. Knock back risen dough; knead briefly and place in centre of tin. Press out to sides; pinch up edges to create a rim.

In a saucepan, cook beef, onion and garlic until meat browns. Season. Add spices and tomato purée (paste). Cook for 10 minutes.

Rinse and mash kidney beans. Stir in any juices from cooked meat. Spread beans over dough. Spoon meat mixture on top.

Arrange tomatoes, sweetcorn and green pepper (capsicum) in circles on top of pizza. Place spring onions in centre. Sprinkle with cheese. Bake in the oven for 20 minutes until golden. Serve with guacamole made by mixing all ingredients smoothly in a blender.

Serves 6-8.

PISSALADIÈRE

1 quantity Traditional Pizza Dough, shaped and ready for topping, see page 8

TOPPING:

440 g (14 oz) can crushed tomatoes

1 onion, chopped

1 clove garlic, crushed

2 tablespoons olive oil

1 tablespoon chopped fresh parsley

2 teaspoons chopped fresh thyme or 1 teaspoon dried thyme

1 tablespoon tomato purée (paste)

1 egg

60 g (2 oz/½ cup) grated Gruyère cheese

salt and pepper

90 g (3 oz) can anchovy fillets

black olives

thyme sprigs and Gruyère cheese, to garnish, if desired

Make the topping. In a saucepan, heat tomatoes, onion, garlic, 1 tablespoon oil, parsley, thyme and tomato purée (paste) together. Bring to the boil, reduce heat; simmer 30 minutes. Cool slightly.

Preheat oven to 200C (400F/Gas 6). Brush dough with remaining oil.

Beat egg and stir into tomato mixture with grated cheese. Spread over dough. Season to taste with salt and pepper. Drain and cut anchovy fillets in thin strips. Arrange in a lattice over pizza. Add olives and bake in the oven for 20 minutes until dough is crisp and golden. Serve garnished with thyme and Gruyère cheese, if desired.

Serves 4.

SPANISH PIZZA

1 quantity Traditional Pizza Dough, shaped and ready for topping, see page 8
TOPPING:
3 skinned chicken breast (fillets), cooked
1 tablespoon olive oil
1 onion, chopped
60 g (2 oz) streaky bacon, chopped
185 g (6 oz/1¼ cups) long-grain rice
125 ml (4 fl oz/½ cup) dry white wine
125 ml (4 fl oz/½ cup) chicken stock
salt and pepper
1 red pepper (capsicum), seeded and chopped
125 g (4 oz) chorizo or garlic sausage, sliced
4 tomatoes, seeded and chopped
few strands saffron, if desired
parsley and chopped pepper (capsicum), to garnish

Make the topping. Cut the chicken into cubes and set aside. In a saucepan, heat oil, add the onion and bacon and fry for 5 minutes. Add rice, wine and stock and season. Bring to the boil, cover and cook for 5 minutes.

Add pepper (capsicum), chorizo or garlic sausage, tomatoes and saffron, if desired. Stir, then cook for 12-15 minutes until rice is tender and most of the liquid has reduced. Stir in chicken.

Meanwhile, preheat oven to 220C (425F/Gas 7). Spoon topping on top of the dough, then bake in the oven for 20 minutes. Serve garnished with parsley and pepper (capsicum).

Serves 6.

SWISS CHEESE PIZZA

1 quantity Traditional Pizza Dough, shaped and ready for topping, see page 8
1 tablespoon vegetable oil
TOPPING:
1 clove garlic, chopped
185 g (6 oz/1½ cups) grated Cheddar cheese
185 g (6 oz/1½ cups) grated Gruyère cheese
2 tablespoons kirsch
freshly grated nutmeg
pepper
red pimento and oregano sprigs, to garnish

Preheat oven to 220C (425F/Gas 7). Brush dough with oil and sprinkle dough with garlic and grated cheeses. Sprinkle with kirsch, nutmeg and pepper. Bake in the oven for 20 minutes until dough is crisp and golden.

Serve the pizza garnished with pimento strips and oregano sprigs.

Serves 6-8.

Variation: Substitute the same quantity of Emmental cheese for the Gruyère cheese, if preferred.

MUSHROOM CALZONI

1 quantity Traditional Pizza Dough, made to end of step 2, see page 8
1 tablespoon olive oil
beaten egg, to glaze
grated Parmesan cheese and oregano sprigs, to garnish
FILLING:
500 g (1 lb) open mushrooms, sliced
2 tablespoons olive oil
1 clove garlic, sliced
salt and pepper
½ teaspoon dried oregano
250 g (8 oz) ricotta or curd cheese
2 tablespoons freshly grated Parmesan cheese

Make the filling. In a saucepan, cook mushrooms in oil with garlic for 3-4 minutes. Remove with a slotted spoon and place in a bowl. Season to taste with salt and pepper; add oregano. Mix in ricotta or curd cheese and Parmesan.

Preheat oven to 220C (425F/ Gas 7). Grease 2 baking sheets. Divide dough into 2 equal pieces. Roll out both pieces on a lightly floured surface to circles measuring 25 cm (10 in) in diameter. Brush lightly with oil.

Divide filling between the 2 pieces of dough, confining it to one half of each circle. Dampen edges with water, then fold over dough to enclose filling and seal well by pressing with a fork. Transfer to baking sheets, brush with beaten egg and make 2 or 3 air holes with a sharp knife. Bake in the oven for 20 minutes until golden. Garnish with grated Parmesan cheese and sprigs of oregano.

Serves 4-6.

LEEK & ONION CALZONI

1 quantity Traditional Pizza dough, made up to end of step 2, see page 8
1 tablespoon olive oil
beaten egg, to glaze
leek, onion and olive slices, to garnish
FILLING:
3 tablespoons olive oil
2 small leeks, sliced
2 onions, sliced
1 large Spanish onion, sliced
125 ml (4 fl oz/½ cup) dry white wine
125 ml (4 fl oz/½ cup) single (light) cream
salt and pepper
freshly grated nutmeg, to taste
125 g (4 oz) stuffed olives, chopped

Make filling. Heat oil and cook leeks and onions gently for 10 minutes until soft. Increase heat, add wine and cook until almost dry.

Reduce heat, add cream and season to taste with salt, pepper and nutmeg. Cook for 2-3 minutes until creamy. Remove from heat, stir in olives and set aside.

Preheat oven to 220C (425F/Gas 7). Grease 2 baking sheets. Divide dough into 2 equal pieces. Roll out both pieces on a lightly floured surface to circles measuring 25 cm (10 in) in diameter. Brush lightly with oil.

Divide filling between the 2 pieces of dough, confining it to one half of each circle. Dampen edges with water, then fold over dough to enclose filling and seal well by pressing with a fork. Transfer to baking sheets, brush with beaten egg and make 2 or 3 air holes with a sharp knife. Bake in the oven for 20 minutes until golden. Serve garnished with leek, onion and olive slices.

Serves 4-6.

CHICKEN LIVER CALZONI

1 quantity Traditional Pizza Dough, made
up to end of step 2, see page 8
1 tablespoon vegetable oil
beaten egg, to glaze
sage leaves, to garnish
FILLING:
60 g (2 oz/¼ cup) butter
500 g (1 lb) chicken livers, trimmed
6 rashers streaky bacon, chopped
1 tablespoon chopped fresh sage
750 g (1½ lb) fresh spinach, trimmed
salt and pepper
few drops lemon juice
freshly grated nutmeg, to taste

Make the filling. In a saucepan,
melt butter and cook chicken livers
quickly until brown but still pink on
the inside. Remove with slotted
spoon and reserve.

Add bacon to saucepan, cook
until brown. Remove with slotted
spoon and add to livers with sage.
Add spinach to saucepan. Cover
and cook until wilted. Drain well,
then chop roughly. Season to taste
with salt and pepper, lemon juice
and nutmeg.

Preheat oven to 220C (425F/Gas
7). Grease 2 baking sheets. Divide
dough into 2 equal pieces. Roll out
both pieces on a lightly floured
surface to circles measuring 25 cm
(10 in) in diameter. Brush lightly
with oil.

Divide filling between the 2
pieces of dough, confining it to one
half of each circle. Dampen edges
with water, then fold over dough to
enclose filling and seal well by pressing with a fork. Transfer to baking
sheets, brush with beaten egg and
make 2 or 3 air holes with a sharp
knife. Bake in the oven for 20
minutes until golden. Serve
garnished with sage leaves.

Serves 4-6.

BROCCOLI CALZONI

1 quantity Deep Pan Pizza Dough, made
up to end of step 1, see page 10
1 teaspoon dried dill weed
1 tablespoon olive oil
beaten egg, to glaze
chopped fresh dill, to garnish
FILLING:
375 g (12 oz) broccoli
250 g (8 oz/2 cups) grated Cheddar cheese
salt and pepper

In a saucepan of boiling water,
blanch broccoli for 2 minutes.
Drain and refresh with cold water.
Drain again. Chop coarsely.

Preheat oven to 220C (425F/Gas
7). Grease 2 baking sheets. Knead
dough with dill weed until evenly
distributed. Divide into 2 equal
pieces. Roll out each piece on a
lightly floured surface to a circle
measuring 25 cm (10 in) in diameter. Brush lightly with oil.

Divide broccoli between the 2
pieces of dough, confining it to one
half of each circle. Sprinkle with
two-thirds of the cheese and season
with salt and pepper. Dampen edges
with water, fold over dough to
enclose filling and seal well by pressing with a fork. Transfer to baking
sheets, brush with beaten egg and
sprinkle with remaining cheese.
Make 2 or 3 air holes with a sharp
knife. Bake in the oven for 20
minutes until golden. Serve the
calzoni garnished with a little
chopped fresh dill.

Serves 4-6.

WATERCRESS PIZZA ROLLS

1 quantity Deep Pan Pizza Dough, made up to end of step 1, see page 10

watercress sprigs, to garnish

FILLING:

30 g (1 oz/6 teaspoons) butter

1 onion, finely chopped

3 bunches watercress, finely chopped

250 g (8 oz) cottage cheese

3 tablespoons grated Parmesan cheese

1 tablespoon lemon juice

1 egg, beaten

salt and pepper

Make the filling. In a saucepan, melt butter and cook onion for 5 minutes until soft. Add chopped watercress and cook for a further 3 minutes. Remove from heat, stir in cottage cheese, 2 tablespoons Parmesan cheese, lemon juice and beaten egg. Season to taste with salt and pepper. Cool and chill until firm.

Grease a baking sheet. Roll out dough on a lightly floured surface to a rectangle measuring about 25 x 35.5 cm (10 x 14 in).

Spread filling evenly over dough leaving a small border clear. Roll up from the long sides to make a firm roll. Seal edges well. Cut into 8-10 slices and arrange on baking sheet. Cover with plastic wrap and leave to rise for about 30 minutes.

Meanwhile, preheat oven to 220C (425F/Gas 7). Sprinkle rolls with remaining Parmesan cheese. Bake in the oven for 20 minutes until dough is crisp and golden. Garnish with watercress.

Serves 4-6.

PIZZA PIPERADE

1 quantity Cornmeal Pizza Dough, made up to end of step 2, see page 8

TOPPING:

6 eggs

salt and pepper

1 orange pepper (capsicum), halved and seeded

1 yellow pepper (capsicum), halved and seeded

2 large or 4 small spring onions

1 tablespoon olive oil

2 tablespoons chopped fresh parsley

pepper (capsicum) rings and parsley sprigs, to garnish

Preheat oven to 200C (400F/Gas 6). Grease a 25 cm (10 in) deep pan pizza tin. Knock back dough, knead briefly on a lightly floured surface.

Place dough in centre of tin, press out to sides with the knuckles.

Beat the eggs together in a bowl with salt and pepper to taste. Set the mixture aside.

Slice peppers (capsicums) into strips, slice spring onions thickly. Heat oil in a saucepan, add peppers and onions and cook for 3 minutes, stirring constantly. Spoon on top of dough. Pour egg mixture on top. Sprinkle with chopped parsley. Bake in the oven for 20 minutes until the egg mixture is set and golden. Serve at once, garnished with pepper (capsicum) rings and parsley sprigs.

Serves 4.

PIZZA RING

1 quantity Traditional Pizza Dough, made up to end of step 2, see page 8
60 g (2 oz/½ cup) freshly grated Parmesan cheese
salt and pepper
FILLING:
75 g (2½ oz) pepper salami, sliced
45 g (1½ oz) smoked cheese
75 g (2½ oz) Mozzarella cheese
45 g (1½ oz) Gruyère cheese
4 slices processed Cheddar cheese
2 hard-boiled eggs
1 tablespoon olive oil
lettuce leaves and cherry tomatoes, to garnish

Grease 22.5 cm (9 in) ring tin. Knock back risen dough, then knead dough with Parmesan cheese and salt and pepper to taste. Roll out on a lightly floured surface to a rectangle measuring 25 x 35.5 cm (10 x 14 in). Chop salami and all the cheeses into small pieces. Mix together.

Sprinkle over surface of dough, leaving a narrow border clear. Halve eggs and cut each half into 3. Arrange in lines from top to bottom across the length of dough. Roll up from the long side and seal edges well.

Coil into a circle and seal ends together. Fit into ring tin. Cover with plastic wrap and leave to stand for 1 hour until dough has risen to just below top of tin. Brush with oil.

Preheat oven to 220C (425F/Gas 7). Bake ring in the oven for 45 minutes until well risen and golden. Serve cold, garnished with lettuce leaves and cherry tomatoes.

Serves 6.

SALMON CALZONCELLI

1 quantity Traditional Pizza Dough, made up to end of step 2, see page 8
TOPPING:
125 g (4 oz) cream cheese
250 g (8 oz) thinly sliced smoked salmon
pepper
juice of ½ lemon
lemon and chives, to garnish

Preheat oven to 200C (400F/Gas 6). Grease 2 baking sheets. Knock back risen dough and knead briefly. Roll out on a lightly floured surface to 0.3 cm (⅛ in) thick. Using a 7.5 cm (3 in) cutter, cut out as many circles as possible. Keep covered with clean cloth while re-rolling dough and cutting out more to make 10-15 in total.

In a bowl, mix cream cheese and smoked salmon together with pepper and lemon juice. Place 1 teaspoon of mixture on one half of each circle. Dampen edges with water, fold over to enclose filling and seal well by pressing with a fork. Transfer to baking sheets and bake for 10-15 minutes until golden. Serve hot or cold, garnished with lemon and chives.

Serves 10-15.

HAM & SALAMI CALZONCELLI

LEAFY GREEN CALZONI

1 quantity Traditional Pizza Dough, made up to end of step 2, see page 8

cress and radish slices, to garnish

FILLING:

60 g (2 oz) sliced ham

60 g (2 oz) sliced salami

60 g (2 oz) Mozzarella cheese

2 tablespoons chopped fresh parsley

1 tablespoon freshly grated Parmesan cheese

1 egg, beaten

salt and pepper

Preheat oven to 200C (400F/Gas 6). Grease 2 baking sheets. Knock back risen dough and knead briefly. Roll out and cut dough as for Salmon Calzoncelli, see page 37.

Chop ham and salami very finely. Place in a bowl. Grate Mozzarella cheese and put in bowl with parsley and Parmesan cheese. Stir in egg and season to taste with salt and pepper. Mix thoroughly.

Place 1 teaspoon of the mixture on one half of each circle. Dampen edges with water, then fold over to enclose filling and seal well by pressing with a fork. Transfer to baking sheets and bake for 15 minutes until golden. Serve hot or cold, garnished with cress and radish slices.

Serves 10-15.

Variation: Chop 90 g (3 oz) mushrooms finely and mix with 6 tablespoons Tomato Topping, see page 12, and 1 tablespoon freshly grated Parmesan cheese. Use as the filling.

1 quantity Traditional Pizza Dough, made up to end of step 2, see page 8

beaten egg, to glaze

tomato slices and marjoram sprigs, to garnish

FILLING:

500 g (1 lb) cabbage or spring greens

3 tablespoons olive oil

2 onions, chopped

440 g (14 oz) can tomatoes, drained

2 cloves garlic, crushed

½ teaspoon dried oregano

salt and pepper

Trim and discard hard stalks from cabbage or spring greens. Wash well and cook in a large saucepan (with just the water that clings to the leaves) for 10-15 minutes until tender. Drain well and chop finely.

Heat 2 tablespoons oil in a saucepan; cook onions until soft. Chop tomatoes, add to pan with garlic and oregano and salt and pepper to taste.

Cook for 20 minutes until thick.

Preheat oven to 220C (425F/Gas 7). Grease 2 baking sheets. Knock back risen dough and knead briefly. Divide dough into 2 equal pieces. Roll out both pieces on a lightly floured surface to circles measuring 25 cm (10 in) in diameter. Lightly brush with remaining oil.

Mix tomato mixture with the cooked greens. Divide between the 2 pieces of dough, confining mixture to one half of each circle. Dampen edges with water. Fold dough over to cover filling and seal well by pressing with a fork. Place on baking sheets, brush with beaten egg and make 2 or 3 air holes with a sharp knife. Bake for 20 minutes until golden. Cut in half. Serve hot, garnished with tomato and marjoram.

Serves 4.

COUNTRY CALZONI

1 quantity Traditional Pizza Dough, made up to end of step 2, see page 8
2 tablespoons olive oil
mushroom slices and thyme sprigs, to garnish
FILLING:
4 large pork sausages with herbs
315 g (10 oz) goat's cheese, such as Chèvre
6-8 dried tomatoes in oil, see Note
125 g (4 oz) mushrooms, sliced
2 dried red chillies, crushed
beaten egg, to glaze

Preheat oven to 220C (425F/Gas 7). Grease 2 baking sheets. Knock back risen dough and knead briefly. Divide dough into 2 equal pieces. Roll both out on a lightly floured surface to circles measuring 25 cm (10 in) in diameter. Brush lightly with oil.

Remove skin from sausages and discard. Break sausagemeat into small pieces and sprinkle over both circles of dough, confining it to one half of circle. Chop cheese roughly and sprinkle over sausagemeat. Cut dried tomatoes into pieces and sprinkle over with mushrooms and crushed chillies.

Fold over dough to enclose filling, dampen edges with water and seal well by pressing with a fork. Transfer to baking sheets, brush with beaten egg and make 2 or 3 air holes with a sharp knife. Bake in the oven for 20 minutes until golden. Serve garnished with mushrooms and thyme.

Serves 4.

Note: Dried tomatoes in oil are available from Italian food shops and delicatessens.

PLUM PIZZA

1 quantity Deep Pan Pizza Dough, made up to end of step 1, see page 10
CUSTARD TOPPING:
7 teaspoons custard powder
4½ teaspoons sugar
315 ml (10 fl oz/1¼ cups) milk
625 g (1¼ lb) plums, halved and stoned
2 tablespoons shredded coconut
TO SERVE:
whipped cream

Preheat oven to 220C (425F/Gas 7). Grease a deep pan pizza tin. Place dough in centre, press to edges with the knuckles, then cover and leave to rise until halfway up the tin.

Meanwhile, make topping. In a bowl, blend custard powder and sugar with a little of the milk until smooth. Heat remaining milk until nearly boiling. Stir into custard powder, then return to pan. Bring to the boil, stirring until thickened. Remove from heat and leave to cool a little.

Slice plum halves into 4 sections. Spoon custard on top of dough. Arrange plum slices on top and sprinkle with coconut. Bake in the oven for 20 minutes. Serve hot or cold with cream.

Serves 4-6.

CHOC-TRUFFLE PIZZA

1 quantity Traditional Pizza Dough, made
up to end of step 3, see page 8

TOPPING:

1 quantity Custard Topping, see page 39

90 g (3 oz) plain chocolate, melted

250 g (8 oz) plain sponge cake crumbs

1 tablespoon apricot jam

90 g (3 oz) white chocolate, melted

60 g (2 oz/½ cup) finely chopped almonds

white chocolate curls, to decorate

Preheat oven to 220C (425F/Gas
7). Bake dough in the oven for 20
minutes until golden. Cool.
    Meanwhile, make topping. In a
bowl, combine custard and melted
dark chocolate. Chill until firm.
    Make truffles, combine cake
crumbs, jam and white chocolate in
a bowl until a stiff paste is formed.
Divide mixture into small balls and
roll in the chopped almonds to
coat.
    To assemble pizza, spread
chocolate-flavoured custard on top
of pizza and arrange truffles around
the edge. Sprinkle with white
chocolate curls.

Serves 6.

RASPBERRY MALLOW PIZZA

1 quantity Crumble Pizza Dough, made up
to end of step 3, see page 10

TOPPING:

3 tablespoons raspberry jam

500 g (1 lb) raspberries

185 g (6 oz) packet marshmallows

few raspberries and raspberry leaves to
decorate, if desired

Preheat oven to 200C (400F/Gas
6). Bake pizza base in the oven for 5
minutes. Remove from oven,
reduce temperature to 180C (350F/
Gas 4).
    In a bowl, beat jam until soft.
Spread over pizza base. Spoon over
raspberries. Arrange marshmallows
over the raspberries. Bake in the
oven for 15-20 minutes until soft.
Allow to cool before serving,
decorated with raspberries and
raspberry leaves, if desired.

Serves 6-8.

TROPICAL PIZZA

1 quantity Traditional Pizza Dough, made up to end of step 3, see page 8

TOPPING:

250 g (8 oz) fresh dates

125 g (4 oz) cream cheese

1 small pineapple

2 kiwi fruit

Preheat oven to 200C (400F/Gas 6). Prick dough with a fork, then bake in the oven for 20 minutes until golden. Leave to cool.

Meanwhile, halve and stone dates. Reserve a few for decoration, then chop the remainder and put in a bowl with the cream cheese. Mix well, then set aside.

Cut top and base from pineapple, then cut off skin. Halve pineapple, slice thinly and cut out hard central core. Peel kiwi fruit; slice thinly.

Spread cream cheese on top of pizza. Arrange slices of pineapple and kiwi on top. Decorate with reserved date halves. Chill until ready to serve.

Serves 6.

BERRY STREUSEL PIZZA

1 quantity Traditional Pizza Dough, made up to end of step 3, see page 8

TOPPING:

125 g (4 oz/1 cup) self-raising flour

90 g (3 oz/⅓ cup) caster sugar

90 g (3 oz/⅓ cup) butter

1 teaspoon ground cinnamon

1 quantity Custard Topping, see page 39

500 g (1 lb) bottled or canned gooseberries, drained

TO SERVE:

cream

Preheat oven to 200C (400F/Gas 6). Prick dough with a fork and bake in the oven for 20 minutes until golden. Allow to cool slightly.

In a bowl, mix flour and sugar, rub in butter until mixture resembles breadcrumbs. Stir in cinnamon and 2 tablespoons water and mix with a fork until a lumpy texture is obtained.

Spoon custard on top of pizza, top with gooseberries, then sprinkle crumble topping over the top. Bake in the oven for 10-15 minutes until light golden. Serve hot with cream.

Serves 6.

CHERRY & ALMOND PIZZA

1 quantity Traditional Pizza Dough, made up to end of step 2, see page 8
30 g (1 oz/2 tablespoons) ground almonds
TOPPING:
2 egg whites
125 g (4 oz/¾ cup) ground almonds
90 g (3 oz/⅓ cup) caster sugar
few drops almond essence
750 g (1½ lb) jar Morello cherries in juice
60 g (2 oz/½ cup) flaked almonds
3 tablespoons Morello cherry jam
icing sugar for dusting
whipped cream, to decorate

Preheat oven to 220C (425F/Gas 7). Knock back risen dough and knead dough with ground almonds. Follow instructions given in step 3, see page 8.

In a bowl, lightly whisk egg whites. Stir in ground almonds, caster sugar and almond essence. Spread the mixture evenly over pizza base.

Drain cherries, reserving juice. Spoon over pizza, reserving a few for decoration. Sprinkle with flaked almonds and bake in the oven for 20 minutes until dough is crisp and golden.

Meanwhile, in a saucepan, heat reserved juice and jam until syrupy. Dust cooked pizza with icing sugar and decorate with whipped cream and reserved cherries. Serve the sauce separately.

Serves 4-6.

APPLE PIE PIZZA

1 quantity Crumble Pizza Dough, made up to end of step 3, see page 10
TOPPING:
3 tablespoons apple and pear spread, see Note
2 tablespoons apple juice or water
3 cooking apples, peeled and cored
60 g (2 oz/2 tablespoons) sultanas
60 g (2 oz/½ cup) chopped walnuts
60 g (2 oz/⅓ cup) soft brown sugar
1 teaspoon ground cinnamon
125 g (4 oz) marzipan
TO SERVE:
apple slices and whipped cream

Preheat oven to 200C (400F/Gas 6). Bake pizza base in the oven for 10 minutes. Remove from oven and then reduce the oven temperature to 180C (350F/Gas 4).

Mix apple and pear spread with apple juice or water to form a soft paste. Spread over pizza base. Slice apples thinly. Place in a bowl with the sultanas, walnuts, sugar and cinnamon. Mix well. Spoon over dough and level surface. Grate marzipan and sprinkle over surface. Bake in the oven for 25-30 minutes. Serve with apple slices and whipped cream.

Serves 6.

Note: Apple and pear spread (called Apple butter in America) is available from most good health food shops.

LEMON MERINGUE PIZZA

1 quantity Traditional Pizza Dough, made up to end of step 3, see page 8

TOPPING:

9 teaspoons cornflour

juice and grated peel 2 lemons

220 g (7 oz/1 cup) caster sugar

2 eggs, separated

star fruit and lemon balm, to decorate

Preheat oven to 200C (400F/Gas 6). Prick dough with a fork and bake in the oven for 20 minutes until golden. Leave to cool slightly. Reduce oven temperature to 180C (350F/Gas 4).

Make topping, place cornflour, lemon juice and peel in a saucepan with 100 ml (3½ fl oz/⅓ cup) water. Bring slowly to the boil, stirring until mixture thickens. Add 125 g (4 oz/½ cup) sugar and the egg yolks, then beat well. Spoon on top of pizza.

In a large bowl, whisk egg whites until stiff. Whisk in half of remaining sugar, then fold in the rest. Pipe or spoon on top of lemon mixture to cover filling completely. Bake in the oven for 10 minutes until meringue is golden. Serve decorated with slices of star fruit and lemon balm leaves.

Serves 6.

CHRISTMAS CALZONI

1 quantity Deep Pan Pizza Dough, made up to end of step 1, see page 10

icing sugar for dusting

FILLING:

125g (4 oz/½ cup) unsalted butter, softened

125 g (4 oz/¾ cup) icing sugar, sifted

125 g (4 oz/⅔ cup) soft brown sugar

1 tablespoon milk

1 tablespoon brandy

6 tablespoons mincemeat

Preheat oven to 220C (425F/Gas 7). Grease 2 baking sheets. Divide dough into 2 equal pieces. Roll out both pieces to circles measuring about 25 cm (10 in) in diameter.

Make the filling. In a bowl, beat butter and sugars together. Gradually stir in milk and brandy until mixture is light and fluffy.

Place 1 tablespoon brandy butter and 3 tablespoons mincemeat to one side of each circle of dough. Brush edges with water, fold over and seal edges firmly. Transfer to baking sheets and bake in the oven for 20 minutes until golden.

Dust with icing sugar. Serve warm with rest of brandy butter.

Serves 4-6.

PEAR & GINGER PIZZA

1 quantity Deep Pan Pizza Dough, shaped and ready for topping, see page 10
TOPPING:
4 pears, peeled and cored
3 tablespoons apple and pear spread
60 g (2 oz/½ cup) chopped walnuts
2 tablespoons chopped crystallized ginger
60 g (1 oz/6 teaspoons) butter, melted
crystallized ginger and angelica, to decorate
TO SERVE:
whipped cream

Preheat oven to 220C (425F/Gas 7). Chop 2 pears and put in a bowl with the apple and pear spread, walnuts and ginger. Mix well, then spread over the dough.

Halve remaining pears. With a sharp knife, slice each half from the rounded end to the point without cutting right through. Fan out the sections and arrange on top of the pizza. Brush with melted butter. Bake in the oven for 20 minutes. Decorate with crystallized ginger and angelica and serve with whipped cream.

Serves 4-6.

BANANA MAPLE SYRUP PIZZA

1 quantity Traditional Pizza Dough, made up to end of step 3, see page 8
TOPPING:
30 g (1 oz/6 teaspoons) butter, melted
4 bananas
2-3 tablespoons maple syrup
60 g (2 oz/½ cup) chopped walnuts
TO SERVE:
whipped cream and maple syrup

Preheat oven to 220C (425F/Gas 7). Brush dough with melted butter.

In a bowl, mash 2 bananas with maple syrup. Spread over pizza base. Slice remaining bananas. Arrange over pizza. Brush with remaining melted butter. Bake in the oven for 20 minutes until dough is crisp and brown.

Sprinkle pizza with chopped walnuts and serve with whipped cream and maple syrup.

Serves 4-6.

ORANGE LIQUEUR PIZZA

1 quantity Deep Pan Pizza Dough, shaped and ready for topping, see page 10

TOPPING:

30 g (1 oz/6 teaspoons) butter, melted, for brushing

3 oranges

2 tablespoons orange liqueur

2 tablespoons orange marmalade

2 tablespoons soft brown sugar

bay leaves, to decorate

Preheat oven to 220C (425F/Gas 7). Brush dough with melted butter.

Using a canelle knife, remove strips of orange peel, set aside for decoration. Peel oranges thinly with a sharp knife or potato peeler. Cut off white pith and discard. Slice oranges thinly. Arrange over dough.

In a pan, heat liqueur, marmalade and sugar until syrupy. Spoon over pizza and bake in the oven for 20 minutes. Meanwhile, blanch peel strips in boiling water for 2-3 minutes. Drain and cool. Decorate pizza with orange peel strips and bay leaves.

Serves 4-6.

BERRY CHEESECAKE PIZZA

1 quantity Crumble Pizza Dough, made to end of step 3, see page 10

TOPPING:

500 g (1 lb) strawberries

375 g (12 oz) curd or low fat cheese

125 ml (4 fl oz/½ cup) milk

grated peel of ½ orange

4 tablespoons orange juice

2 tablespoons clear honey

1 egg, beaten

2 tablespoons redcurrant jelly

whipped cream and strawberry leaves, to decorate

Preheat oven to 190C (375F/Gas 5). Bake dough in the oven for 15 minutes. Meanwhile, hull and chop half the strawberries. In a bowl, blend curd or low fat cheese with milk, orange peel, orange juice, honey and egg.

Spoon chopped strawberries over pizza base. Spoon cheese mixture on top and smooth over. Bake in the oven for 35-40 minutes. Switch off the oven, open the door and allow the cheesecake to cool gradually.

In a saucepan, heat redcurrant jelly until melted. Arrange reserved strawberries on top of cheesecake. Brush with melted jelly. Serve decorated with whipped cream and strawberry leaves.

Serves 4-6.

PANETTONE

30 g (1 oz/6 teaspoons) fresh (compressed) yeast, or 2 tablespoons dried active yeast

90 ml (3 fl oz/⅓ cup) hand-hot water

60 g (2 oz/⅓ cup) sugar

4 egg yolks

few drops vanilla essence

grated peel of 1 lemon

375 g (12 oz/3 cups) strong white flour

½ teaspoon salt

90 g (3 oz/⅓ cup) butter, softened

60 g (2 oz/⅓ cup) chopped candied peel

45 g (1½ oz/2 tablespoons) raisins

45 g (1½ oz/2 tablespoons) sultanas

60 g (2 oz/¼ cup) butter, melted, for brushing

In a small bowl, cream fresh yeast with water; put in warm place until frothy. If using dried active yeast, whisk with 1 teaspoon of sugar and the water; leave until frothy.

In a large bowl, put sugar, egg yolks, essence and lemon peel. Stir in yeast mixture. Mix flour with salt. Gradually add two-thirds flour to yeast mixture, until a sticky dough is obtained.

Divide butter into 3 equal pieces. Add one piece at a time, kneading until mixture is heavy and stringy. Add remaining flour; mix well. Knead on a lightly floured surface until firm and oily, but not sticky. Place in a bowl. Cover, set aside for 1½ hours until doubled.

Preheat oven to 200C (400F/Gas 6). Well grease a charlotte tin. Knead peel, raisins and sultanas into dough. Place in tin, cover, leave to rise to just below top of tin.

Brush with melted butter; bake for 10 minutes. Reduce temperature to 180C (350F/Gas 4). Brush again with butter; bake for 30-40 minutes. Brush with more butter after 15 minutes. Leave to cool.

Serves 10-12.

GRAPE BREAD

1 quantity Deep Pan Pizza Dough, made up to end of step 1, see page 10

30 g (1 oz/5 teaspoons) caster sugar

FILLING:

375 g (12 oz) red seedless grapes

60 g (2 oz/¼ cup) caster sugar

TO SERVE:

extra sugar and pouring cream

Preheat oven to 220C (425F/Gas 7). Grease a 25 cm (10 in) deep pan pizza tin or sandwich tin.

Spread grapes on a baking sheet and bake in the oven for 10 minutes. Meanwhile knock back risen dough and knead with 30 g (1 oz/5 teaspoons) caster sugar. Divide into 2 equal pieces. Roll each piece to a circle measuring 25 cm (10 in) in diameter. Remove grapes from oven; turn off oven.

Place one dough circle in tin. Brush surface with water and spoon over half the grapes. Sprinkle with half the remaining sugar. Lay second piece of dough on top and press gently with fingertips to seal dough around grapes and make small pockets.

Spoon remaining grapes over the surface and sprinkle with remaining sugar. Cover with plastic wrap and leave to rise for 1½ hours. Preheat oven to 200C (400F/Gas 6). Bake in the oven for 20-25 minutes until golden. Cool, then dust with extra sugar and serve with cream.

Serves 4-6.

BREAD STICKS

1 quantity Traditional Pizza Dough, made up to end of step 2, see page 8

sesame or poppy seeds, or cracked or kibbled wheat, to sprinkle

TO SERVE:

slices of prosciutto (Parma ham), if desired

Preheat oven to 200 C (400F/Gas 6). Grease several baking sheets.

Knock back risen dough and knead briefly. Divide dough into approximately 18 equal-sized pieces and roll each piece to a 20 cm (8 in) length. Arrange on baking sheets and brush with water.

Leave plain or sprinkle with sesame or poppy seeds, or cracked or kibbled wheat, if desired. Bake in the oven for 15-20 minutes until crisp and golden. Allow to cool before serving plain or wrapped with slices of prosciutto (Parma ham), if desired, to serve as a cocktail snack.

Makes about 18.

POLENTA BREAD

| 220 g (7 oz/1⅓ cups) coarse ground cornmeal |
| 125 g (4 oz/1 cup) plain flour |
| 1 heaped teaspoon salt |
| ¼ teaspoon black pepper |
| 3 tablespoons olive oil |
| 220 ml (7 fl oz/1 cup) hand-hot water |
| TO SERVE: |
| salad |

Preheat oven to 220 C (425F/Gas 7). Grease a 30 cm (12 in) pizza tin.

In a bowl, mix together the cornmeal and flour and season with salt and pepper. In a jug, whisk together 2 tablespoons oil and hand-hot water. Stir into the flour and mix with a fork to form a grainy paste.

Place in centre of tin and press to edges with the knuckles. Prick with a fork and brush with remaining oil. Bake in the oven for 20 minutes until golden. Serve the bread warm with salad.

Serves 4-6.

FOCACCIA

1 quantity Traditional Pizza Dough, made up to end of step 2, see page 8

1 teaspoon crushed dried rosemary

about 18 stoned green olives

coarse sea salt, to sprinkle

rosemary sprigs, to garnish

Preheat oven to 220C (425F/Gas 7). Grease a 30 cm (12 in) pizza tin.

Knock back risen dough and knead dough with crushed rosemary. Place dough in centre of tin and press to edges with knuckles. Prick all over with a fork. Press olives into dough. Brush with water and sprinkle with sea salt. Bake in the oven for 20 minutes until crisp and golden, Serve garnished with rosemary.

Serves 4-6.

Variations: Omit green olives and instead knead chopped black olives into dough with rosemary.

Or knead 60 g (2 oz/½ cup) freshly grated Parmesan cheese into dough and season to taste with a little black pepper. In both cases, prick dough with a fork, brush with water and, if desired, sprinkle with sea salt before cooking.

PIADINA

345 g (11 oz/2½ cups) strong white plain flour

1 heaped teaspoon salt

½ teaspoon baking powder

75 ml (2½ fl oz/⅓ cup) milk

3 tablespoons olive oil

TO SERVE:

salami, cheese and salad

In a bowl, mix flour with salt and baking powder. Mix milk with 75 ml (2½ fl oz/⅓ cup) water. Add oil and a little of the water and milk mixture to flour mixture. Stir with a fork and gradually add more liquid until it has all been incorporated. Mix to form a soft dough.

Turn onto a lightly floured surface and knead until smooth. Allow to rest for 15 minutes. Divide dough into 12 equal pieces. Roll each piece out to a circle measuring 7.5 cm (3 in) in diameter.

Heat a heavy-based frying pan or griddle until a drop of water flicked on the surface bounces and evaporates. Place 2-3 circles in pan or on griddle and cook for 30 seconds. Flip over and continue cooking.

Turn each circle 2 or 3 times until sides are speckled with brown. Place on wire rack while cooking remainder. Serve warm with salami, cheese and salad.

Serves 4-6.

PASTA

TYPES OF PASTA

There are dozens of different types of pasta and some are more suited to a particular dish than others, but pasta of a similar shape may be substituted in any of the recipes in this book.

The secret of cooking pasta successfully is to use plenty of water. Allow 1.2 litres (2 pints/4¾ cups) for every 125 g (4 oz) pasta. Bring the water to the boil, add 3 teaspoons oil and 3 teaspoons salt to each 500 g (1 lb) pasta. Then add the pasta. Long pasta such as spaghetti should be fanned out slowly into the water as it softens. Bring back to the boil and continue boiling until the pasta is cooked. To test whether it is done, remove a piece from the water and bite into it. It should be *al dente*, or slightly firm. If the pasta is to be cooked again in a baked dish, undercook it slightly, as it will continue to cook in the oven.

Drain the pasta in a colander, shaking to remove most of the water, but leave a little water clinging to it to prevent it from sticking. Pour the pasta into a warmed serving dish and toss with a little olive oil, butter or some of the sauce which accompanies it. If the pasta is to be served in a salad or reheated in a baked dish, it may be rinsed in cold water and drained.

The cooking times for pasta vary according to its size and shape. Follow the directions below as a guideline for dried pasta, but keep testing during the cooking time, to avoid overcooking. Wholewheat pasta takes longer, and fresh pasta much less time to cook than ordinary dried pasta.

Lasagne (1) Cooking time: Some lasagne requires no pre-cooking and is layered straight into a dish with sauce and baked in the oven. Other lasagne must be boiled for 10 minutes before being layered with other ingredients.
Uses: Layered with meat, fish or vegetable sauces. May also be rolled round filling, like cannelloni.

Pappardelle (2) Cooking time: 8 minutes.
Uses: Traditionally served with hare sauce.

Tagliatelle (3) and Fettucine (4) Cooking time: 6 minutes.
Uses: Similar to spaghetti, but particularly good with creamy sauces which adhere better than heavy sauces. May also be fried.

Spaghetti (5) Cooking time: 12 minutes.
Uses: Served simply with butter or oil, or with almost any kind of sauce.

Spaghettini (6) Cooking time: 8 minutes.
Uses: Traditionally served with fish and shellfish sauces. Also good with tomato sauce.

Vermicelli (7) Cooking time: 5 minutes.
Uses: Very thin vermicelli sold in clusters is ideal for serving with very light sauces. Long vermicelli is used in the same way as spaghetti.

Macaroni (8) and Bucatini (9) Cooking time: 8-10 minutes.
Uses: Often used in baked dishes, particularly those with a cheese-based sauce.

Rigatoni (10) Cooking time: 10 minutes.
Uses: Generally used in baked dishes. The ridges help the sauce to cling to the pasta. It may also be stuffed.

Penne (11) Cooking time: 10 minutes.
Uses: Served with meat sauces, which catch in the hollows.

Cannelloni (12) Cooking time: Most cannelloni tubes require no pre-cooking and are stuffed directly before baking. If they are to be fried, they should be boiled first for about 7-10 minutes.
Uses: Filled cannelloni may be baked

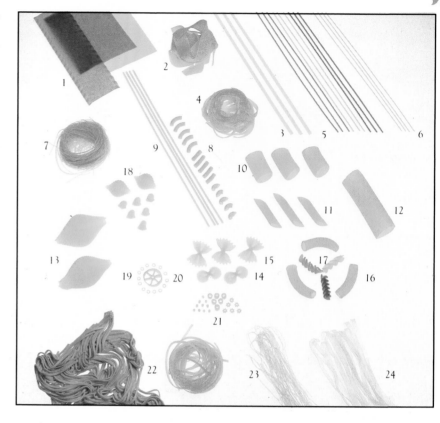

in the oven in a sauce, or topped with butter and grated cheese, and may also be deep-fried until crisp.

Conchiglie (13) Cooking time: Large shells take about 15 minutes to cook and smaller ones 10 minutes.
Uses: Large shells may be stuffed, and their shape makes a fish filling particularly appropriate. Smaller shells are used in casseroles and soup, and served cold in salads.

Fiochetti (bows) (14) and Farfalle (butterflies) (15) Cooking time: 10 minutes.
Uses: Ideal for serving with meat or vegetable sauces, which become trapped in the folds.

Fusilli (16) and Tortiglioni (spirals) (17) Cooking time: 10 minutes.
Uses: Served with substantial meat sauces, which are trapped in the twists. Also good in salads.

Lumache (18) Cooking time: 10 minutes.
Uses: Similar to conchiglie.

Rotini (wheels) (19) and Anelli (20) Cooking time: 8 minutes.
Uses: Added to savoury bakes and salads.

Pastina (anellini, ditalini, stellini) (21) Cooking time: 8 minutes.
Uses: Most often added to soups, but may be used in other dishes.

Egg Noodles (22) Cooking time: 4-5 minutes.
Uses: Flat noodles are often served in soups. Round ones are served in sauces, and are best for stir-frying. Also served as an accompaniment instead of rice.

Rice Noodles (23) Cooking time: Simply soak in hot water for 10-15 minutes.
Uses: Served in spicy sauces, soups and stir-fry dishes.

Transparent (Cellophane) Noodles (24) Cooking time: Soak in hot water for 5 minutes.
Uses: Added to soups or deep-fried as a garnish.

PASTA VERDE
Cook 125 g (4 oz) spinach, then drain, squeeze out as much moisture as possible and chop very finely. Add spinach to eggs and flour, adding extra flour if necessary.

2 eggs
185 g (6 oz/1½ cups) strong white bread flour
pinch of salt

Any quantity of pasta may be made by using the proportions of 1 egg to 90 g (3 oz/¾ cup) flour, but the most convenient quantity for a beginner to handle is a 2 or 3-egg mixture. Larger amounts should be mixed and rolled in batches.

TOMATO PASTA
Add 3 teaspoons tomato purée (paste) to the eggs and flour.

Beat eggs in a large bowl. Sift flour and salt into bowl. Mix together with a fork, then press with the hands to form a solid piece of dough. It should be firm but pliable, and not sticky. Add more flour if it seems too moist.

HERB PASTA
Add 3 teaspoons of a single chopped fresh herb, such as parsley, or mixed fresh herbs to the eggs and flour.

Turn dough onto a lightly floured surface and knead firmly for 5-10 minutes until smooth. Wrap in a damp tea towel and leave to rest for 30 minutes at room temperature.

WHOLEWHEAT PASTA
Use wholewheat bread flour instead of white flour, or for a lighter texture, use a mixture of wholewheat and white flour.

ROLLING DOUGH BY HAND

To roll pasta dough by hand, you need a long rolling pin and a large, clean work surface. It is essential to work quickly or the pasta will dry out and crack. Lightly flour the work surface. Press the dough flat with your hands and roll it out firmly with the rolling pin. Starting from the centre, roll away from you. Keep lifting the sheet of pasta on the rolling pin and turning it 45 degrees. As you roll, lift the far edge on the rolling pin and push it away from you to stretch the dough.

As the sheet of pasta becomes larger, allow it to hang over the edge of the table to increase the stretch. Eventually the sheet of pasta should look smooth and suede-like in texture, and be so thin that you can read newsprint through it!

However, as the sheet of pasta becomes large, it becomes more difficult to turn and unless you are an expert, you will not be able to roll it as thinly by hand as with a machine. In some cases you may find you need a slightly larger quantity of pasta than that given in a recipe.

If making lasagne or filled pasta, such as ravioli or tortellini, the pasta should be used immediately. Otherwise it should be spread out on a tea towel and left to dry for 30 minutes. Turn it over after 15 minutes. Leave to dry enough to prevent it sticking, but not so much that it becomes brittle. The dough is then ready for cutting into shapes.

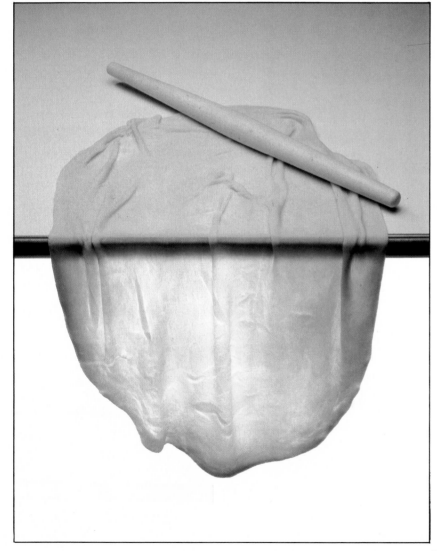

CUTTING PASTA SHAPES

TAGLIATELLE
Loosely roll up the pasta dough into a cylinder. Using a sharp knife, cut the cylinder into even widths. Shake out the coils into loose nests. These may be cooked straight away or left to dry for several days before being stored.

LASAGNE & CANNELLONI
Using a sharp knife or serrated pasta-cutting wheel, cut lasagne sheets to whatever size will best fit your dish. For most purposes, sheets measuring 10 x 12 cm (4 x 5 in) are the most convenient. For cannelloni, cut pasta as for lasagne. The sheets can then be cooked and rolled round a stuffing before baking in the oven.

PAPPARDELLE & FARFALLE
For pappardelle, using a serrated pasta-cutting wheel, cut pasta into strips 2 cm (¾ in) wide and 30 cm (12 in) long. For farfalle, cut pasta sheet into 5 cm (2 in) squares with pasta-cutting wheel. Pinch each square together in the middle to produce a butterfly effect.

Note: Cut pasta trimmings into pretty shapes with a biscuit or aspic cutter. Use for garnishing soups.

PASTA MACHINES

Electric machines are available which mix the dough and then extrude it through a selected cutter to give a variety of shapes, but unless you intend to make large quantities of pasts on a regular basis, a machine is not essential.

The pasta dough can either be made by hand, see page 51, or it can be mixed in a food processor. To make it in a food processor, break the eggs into the bowl and process for 30 seconds, then add the sifted flour and salt and process until the mixture forms a ball.

Rolling pasta in a machine

Rolling pasta dough in a machine is much quicker and easier than rolling it by hand.

The most useful machine is a hand cranking one that rolls the pasta dough into sheets. The space between the rollers is reduced until the dough is thin enough to use, see opposite. The sheets are then passed through cutters of different widths.

Different cutters

By fitting cutters of various sizes onto the pasta rolling machine, it is possible to cut spaghetti or noodles in several different widths.

When cutting spaghetti, it is important not to use very long sheets of pasta, otherwise they tend to stick together. Once the dough is cut into long strands, they need to be left to dry before using. Place a tea towel over the back of a chair and spread out the pasta. Leave to dry for about 30 minutes.

ROLLING DOUGH IN A MACHINE

Divide dough into as many pieces as the number of eggs used. Set the rollers of the machine to the widest setting. Flatten the pieces of dough and roll each piece through the machine.

Fold each piece into 3 crosswise and feed it though again. Repeat about 7 times until the sheet of pasta is smooth and silky. Set rollers one notch closer together and feed pasta through once only. Keep setting rollers closer together and feed pasta through once on each setting.

Cut sheets of pasta in half if they become too long to handle easily. A final rolling on narrowest but one setting should produce pasta of correct thickness for most purposes.

MAKING FILLED PASTA

ROUND RAVIOLI
This is made by cutting circles from the filled sheets of pasta, using a sharp knife, serrated pasta-cutting wheel or a special round pasta-cutting stamp.

RAVIOLI
Prepare filling first and set it aside. Make the pasta dough, see page 51, and roll it into strips. Lay the strips out on a tea towel or floured surface. Keep covered with a damp cloth while filling a few at a time.

HALF MOON RAVIOLI
Cut circles about 5 cm (2 in) in diameter. Place a pea-sized amount of filling in the middle. Fold over one side of the circle and press edges firmly together. Leave to dry as for ravioli.

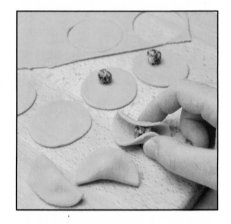

Place small mounds (about ½ teaspoon) of filling at 4 cm (1½ in) intervals over one sheet of pasta and lay a second sheet over the top.

TORTELLINI
Cut circles about 5 cm (2 in) in diameter. Place a pea-sized amount of filling slightly to one side of the middle. Fold over one side of the circle so that it falls just short of the other side. Press edges firmly together. Curve the semi-circle round and pinch edges together. Leave to dry as for ravioli.

Press down firmly between the mounds of pasta and cut between the mounds with a pasta-cutting wheel. Spread the ravioli out on a tea towel to dry for about 30 minutes, turning them over after 15 minutes. Take care to keep them separate or they will stick together.

CAPPELLETTI
Cut 5 cm (2 in) squares of pasta. Put a small amount of filling in centre of each square. Fold in half diagonally to form a triangle, leaving a slight overlap between edges. Press firmly to seal. Wrap 1 long side of triangle round a finger until the 2 ends overlap. Press ends firmly together, with points of the triangle upright. Leave to dry as for ravioli.

MINESTRONE SOUP

9 teaspoons olive oil

4 rashers streaky bacon, cut into matchsticks

1 onion, chopped

2 carrots, chopped

2 sticks celery, chopped

250 g (8 oz) white cabbage, roughly shredded

1 courgette (zucchini), diced

125 g (4 oz) French beans, cut into 2.5 cm (1 in) lengths

1.5 litres (2½ pints/6 cups) chicken stock

440 g (14 oz) can tomatoes

salt and pepper

125 g (4 oz/¾ cup) macaroni

3 teaspoons chopped fresh parsley

freshly grated Parmesan cheese, to serve

In a large saucepan, heat olive oil. Add bacon, onion, carrots and celery. Cook gently until beginning to soften.

Add cabbage, courgette (zucchini), beans, stock and tomatoes and season with salt and pepper. Bring to the boil, cover and simmer for about 2 hours.

Add macaroni. Cook for a further 10-15 minutes until macaroni is tender. Add parsley. Serve with Parmesan cheese handed separately.

Serves 6-8.

Variation: Vary the vegetables according to taste and availability. Soaked haricot beans may be added at the beginning of the cooking time. Pesto, see page 64, may be stirred in before serving. Add to taste.

WHITE ONION SOUP

60 g (2 oz/¼ cup) butter

3 onions, finely sliced

3 teaspoons plain flour

315 ml (10 fl oz/1¼ cups) boiling water

940 ml (30 fl oz/3¾ cups) milk

60 g (2 oz/⅔ cup) straight vermicelli, broken into 1 cm (½ in) pieces

salt and pepper

bacon rolls and sprigs of parsley, to garnish

In a saucepan, melt butter. Add onions. Cook gently until soft.

Stir in flour. Gradually add boiling water. Cook, stirring, until smooth and thickened. Stir in milk.

Bring to the boil. Add vermicelli and season with salt and pepper. Cover pan. Cook, stirring frequently, until vermicelli is tender. Serve in individual bowls, garnished with bacon rolls and sprigs of parsley.

Serves 4-6.

TOMATO & PASTA SOUP

8 tomatoes

60 g (2 oz / ¼ cup) butter

1 onion, finely chopped

60 g (2 oz / ⅓ cup) ditalini or elbow macaroni

1 litre (32 fl oz / 4 cups) chicken stock

pinch of saffron powder

pinch of chilli powder

salt

sprigs of parsley, to garnish

Put tomatoes in a bowl. Pour over boiling water. Leave for 1 minute, then drain. Pour over cold water.

Leave for 1 minute, then drain. Remove the skins and chop the tomato flesh.

In a saucepan, melt butter. Add onion. Cook until beginning to soften. Add ditalini or macaroni and cook for 2 minutes, stirring.

Add tomatoes, stock and saffron. Bring to boil. Cover and simmer until pasta is tender. Stir in chilli powder and salt to taste. Pour soup into individual bowls and garnish with a sprig of parsley.

Serves 4.

LIGHT VEGETABLE SOUP

940 ml (30 fl oz / 3¾ cups) vegetable stock, made from vegetable trimmings or stock cube

2 carrots, peeled

2 sticks celery, thinly sliced

90 g (3 oz) button mushrooms, thinly sliced

60 g (2 oz / ¾ cup) frozen peas

30 g (1 oz / 2 tablespoons) small pasta shells

salt and pepper

1 tablespoon chopped fresh parsley

Put stock into a saucepan and bring to the boil.

With the pointed end of a potato peeler, cut grooves down carrots. Cut into thin slices. Add to stock with celery, mushrooms, peas and pasta.

Bring to the boil, then cover pan and simmer for about 15 minutes, or until pasta and vegetables are tender. Season with salt and pepper to taste. Pour the soup into individual bowls and sprinkle the chopped parsley over the top of each portion,

Serves 4.

BEAN & PASTA SOUP

6 teaspoons olive oil

1 onion, finely chopped

1 clove garlic, crushed

2 carrots, finely chopped

2 sticks celery, finely chopped

1.5 litres (2½ pints/6 cups) chicken stock

salt and pepper

90 g (3 oz/1½ cups) pasta shells

440 g (14 oz) can borlotti beans

celery leaves, to garnish

In a large saucepan, heat oil. Add onion, garlic, carrots and celery and cook gently until soft.

Add chicken stock and season with salt and pepper. Bring to the boil, cover and simmer for 20 minutes. Add pasta and cook for a further 10 minutes, or until pasta is tender.

Drain beans. Rinse in cold water. Sieve half the beans, or process in a blender or food processor. Add puréed and whole beans to soup. Stir well. Cook for 2 minutes to heat through. Serve in individual bowls, garnished with celery leaves.

Serves 6-8.

AVGOLEMONO SOUP

1 litre (1¾ pints/4 cups) chicken stock

45 g (1½ oz/⅓ cup) pastini

salt and pepper

2 eggs

juice of 1 lemon

lemon slices and sprigs of mint, to garnish

In a saucepan, heat chicken stock. Bring to the boil. Add pastini and season to taste with salt and pepper. Cook for 5 minutes until pastini is tender.

In a bowl, beat eggs. Add lemon juice and beat to mix thoroughly. Pour a ladleful of hot stock onto the beaten eggs, whisking them continuously.

Pour egg mixture into stock in saucepan. Over a very low heat, whisk continuously for 3-4 minutes without boiling until soup thickens slightly. Pour into individual bowls and garnish with lemon slices and sprigs of mint.

Serves 4.

SMOKED SALMON ROULADE

3 sheets lasagne
1 bunch watercress, washed and trimmed
3 spring onions, very finely chopped
3 teaspoons olive oil
1 teaspoon horseradish sauce
salt and pepper
1 avocado
juice of ½ a lemon
90 g (3 oz) smoked salmon
60 ml (2 fl oz/¼ cup) mayonnaise
60 ml (2 fl oz/¼ cup) crème fraîche
1 tablespoon chopped fresh dill weed
lemon slice and sprig of dill, to garnish

In a large saucepan of boiling salted water, cook pasta until just tender. Drain, rinse in cold water, then pat dry.

In a saucepan of boiling water, blanch watercress for 10 seconds. Drain and refresh in a bowl of cold water. Squeeze gently in a cloth to dry, then chop finely.

In a bowl, mix together water-cress, spring onions, olive oil, horse-radish sauce, salt and pepper. Peel, halve and stone avocado. Cut into slices lengthwise. Toss in lemon juice.

Spread a little watercress mixture over each sheet of lasagne. Lay a slice of smoked salmon on each sheet. Arrange slices of avocado in a line down the length of the middle of each sheet.

Starting with a long side of pasta, roll up Swiss roll fashion. Wrap each roll in plastic wrap. Chill for 2 hours. In a bowl, mix together mayonnaise, crème fraîche and dill weed, salt and pepper. Add a little milk, if necessary, to make a pouring consistency. Cut each roll diagonally into slices 2 cm/¾ in wide. Garnish with lemon slice and sprig of dill and serve with dill sauce.

Serves 4-6 as a first course.

SEAFOOD PASTA SALAD

375 g (12 oz) monkfish
60 ml (2 fl oz/¼ cup) dry white wine
250 g (8 oz/4 cups) green pasta spirals
90 g (3 oz) smoked salmon trout
125 g (4 oz/¾ cup) peeled prawns
2 teaspoons chopped fresh dill weed
lemon slices and sprigs of dill, to garnish
SALAD DRESSING:
½ teaspoon Dijon mustard
salt and pepper
1 clove garlic, crushed
3 teaspoons lemon juice
75 ml (2½ fl oz/⅓ cup) olive oil

Cut monkfish into cubes. Put into a saucepan with wine and sufficient water to cover. Cook for a few minutes until fish is tender. Drain, then leave to cool.

In a large saucepan of boiling salted water, cook pasta spirals until tender. Drain and rinse with cold water.

Cut salmon trout into strips. In a bowl, combine monkfish, salmon trout, prawns, pasta and dill weed.

To make dressing, in a bowl mix together mustard, salt, pepper, garlic and lemon juice. Gradually stir in olive oil. Pour dressing over pasta mixture. Mix well. Serve, garnished with lemon and dill.

Serves 4-6.

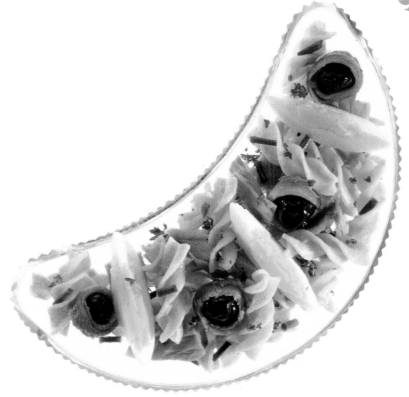

THREE-WAY PASTA SALAD

6 spring onions

1 small red pepper (capsicum)

1 small green pepper (capsicum)

1 quantity salad dressing, see page 58

250 g (8 oz/4 cups) red, green and
white pasta shells

Chop spring onions finely. Cut peppers (capsicums) into quarters. Remove seeds, cut into small dice. In a bowl, combine spring onions and peppers (capsicums) with salad dressing.

In a large saucepan of boiling salted water, cook pasta until just tender. Drain, rinse in cold water, then drain thoroughly.

In a serving bowl, mix together dressing and pasta shells.

Serves 4-6.

PASTA NIÇOISE

250 g (8 oz/4 cups) wholewheat
pasta spirals

6 canned anchovies, drained

30 g (1 oz/2 tablespoons) black olives

220 g (7 oz) can tuna fish

3 teaspoons chopped fresh parsley

3 teaspoons chopped fresh chives
or mint

wedges of hard-boiled egg, to
garnish

DRESSING:

salt and pepper

1 teaspoon Dijon mustard

1 clove garlic, crushed

3 teaspoons wine vinegar

75 ml (2½ fl oz/⅓ cup) olive oil

In a large saucepan of boiling salted water, cook pasta spirals until just tender. Drain, rinse in cold water, then drain thoroughly.

Cut each anchovy in half lengthwise. Wrap fillets around olives. Drain tuna fish. In a large bowl, combine pasta, flaked tuna fish, olives, parsley and chives or mint.

To make dressing, in a bowl mix together salt, pepper, mustard, garlic and vinegar. Gradually stir in olive oil. Pour dressing over pasta mixture. Mix thoroughly. Garnish with egg.

Serves 4.

— CHICKEN TARRAGON SALAD —

250 g (8 oz/4 cups) pasta shells
1.5 kg (3 lb) chicken, cooked
250 g (8 oz) seedless grapes
1 tablespoon chopped fresh tarragon
60 ml (2 fl oz/¼ cup) mayonnaise
60 ml (2 fl oz/¼ cup) crème fraîche
salt and pepper
sprigs of parsley, to garnish

In a large saucepan of boiling salted water, cook pasta shells until just tender. Drain, rinse in cold water, then drain again thoroughly.

Remove meat from chicken and cut into pieces. In a bowl, mix together pasta, chicken, grapes and tarragon.

In a bowl, mix together mayonnaise and crème fraîche. Season with salt and pepper. Pour over chicken and mix thoroughly. Serve salad at room temperature garnished with a few sprigs of parsley.

Serves 6

— AVOCADO PASTA SALAD —

250 g (8 oz/4 cups) pasta bows
1 large avocado
grated peel and juice of ½ an orange
salt and pepper
orange twists and peel, smoked salmon cornets and sprigs of dill, to garnish

In a large saucepan of boiling salted water, cook pasta bows. Drain, rinse in cold water then drain thoroughly.

Cut avocado in half and remove stone. Scoop out flesh, taking care to scrape all the dark green flesh from the skin. Put avocado, orange peel and juice, salt and pepper into a blender or food processor. Purée until smooth.

In a large bowl, combine avocado purée and pasta. Mix until pasta is coated with avocado purée. Garnish with orange twists and peel, smoked salmon cornets and sprigs of dill.

Serves 6 as an accompaniment to other dishes.

Note: This salad should be served soon after making, otherwise the avocado will discolour.

Variations: Add peeled prawns or chopped smoked salmon to make an elegant first course.

— CREAMY MUSHROOM SAUCE —

90 g (3 oz/⅓ cup) butter
125 g (4 oz) mushrooms, sliced
155 ml (5 fl oz/⅔ cup) crème fraîche
2 egg yolks
60 g (2 oz/½ cup) grated Parmesan cheese
salt and pepper
pinch of freshly grated nutmeg
125 g (4 oz/1 cup) frozen peas, thawed
sprig of mint, to garnish

In a frying pan, melt 30 g (1 oz/6 teaspoons) butter. Add mushrooms and cook gently until tender. Set aside. In a bowl, beat together crème fraîche, egg yolks, Parmesan cheese, salt, pepper and nutmeg until well combined.

In a saucepan, melt remaining butter. Stir in crème fraîche mixture. Add peas and mushrooms. Over a very low heat, cook gently, stirring, until mixture is heated through and beginning to thicken slightly. Serve at once over pasta, garnished with a sprig of mint.

Serves 4.

— MASCARPONE SAUCE —

15 g (½ oz/3 teaspoons) butter
250 g (8 oz/1 cup) mascarpone
milk (see recipe)
90 g (3 oz/¾ cup) walnuts, coarsely chopped
30 g (1 oz/¼ cup) grated Parmesan cheese
salt and pepper

In a saucepan, melt butter. Gradually stir in mascarpone.

Heat gently, stirring until sauce is smooth. Add a little milk if necessary, to give a smooth, creamy consistency.

Stir in walnuts and Parmesan cheese. Season with salt and pepper. Serve at once with spaghetti or tagliatelle.

Serves 4.

CHICKEN LIVER SAUCE

30 g (1 oz / 6 teaspoons) butter
4 rashers bacon, rinds removed chopped
1 onion, finely chopped
1 clove garlic, crushed
375 g (12 oz) chicken livers, chopped
2 teaspoons plain flour
185 ml (6 fl oz / ¾ cup) chicken stock
1 teaspoon tomato purée (paste)
salt and pepper
1 teaspoon chopped fresh marjoram
60 ml (2 fl oz / ¼ cup) thick sour cream
sprigs of marjoram, to garnish

In a saucepan, melt butter. Add bacon, onion and garlic. Cook until onion is soft.

Stir in chicken livers. Cook, stirring, until livers are no longer pink. Stir in flour.

Gradually stir in the chicken stock. Add tomato purée (paste), salt, pepper and marjoram. Cover. Cook gently for 10 minutes. Stir in cream. Serve in a sauceboat, garnished with sprigs of marjoram, or poured over pasta, such as rigatoni.

Serves 4.

HARE SAUCE

saddle of hare, weighing about
500 g (1 lb)
6 teaspoons vegetable oil
6 rashers bacon, rinds removed, chopped
1 onion, finely chopped
1 carrot, finely chopped
2 teaspoons plain flour
155 ml (5 fl oz / ⅔ cup) meat stock
salt and pepper
freshly grated nutmeg
MARINADE:
250 ml (8 fl oz / 1 cup) red wine
1 onion, sliced
1 stick celery, sliced
1 bay leaf
2 black peppercorns

Put hare into a bowl. Mix together marinade ingredients and pour over hare. Cover bowl. Leave to marinate, in a cool place, for 1-2 days.

In a saucepan, heat oil. Add bacon, onion and carrot. Cook gently until onion is soft. Remove hare from marinade, add to pan and brown all over. Stir in flour. Strain marinade; gradually add to pan with stock. Season with salt, pepper and nutmeg.

Cover pan and cook over a gentle heat for 1½ hours, or until hare is very tender. Remove hare from pan. Cut all meat off the bones and cut into small pieces. Return meat to pan and stir into sauce.

Serves 4.

Note: This sauce is traditionally served with pappardelle, wide ribbon pasta. Garnish with bay leaves.

SHELLFISH SAUCE

60 ml (2 fl oz/¼ cup) olive oil
500 g (1 lb) fresh mussels in shells, cleaned
1 clove garlic, crushed
2 shallots, finely chopped
185 ml (6 fl oz/⅔ cup) dry white wine
salt and pepper
250 g (8 oz) can clams
6 teaspoons chopped fresh parsley

In a large saucepan, heat half the olive oil. Add mussels. Cover and cook for about 4 minutes until all mussels are open.

Heat remaining oil in pan. Add garlic and shallots. Cook until shallots are soft. Drain mussels. Strain cooking liquid; add to shallots with white wine. Season with salt and pepper. Bring to the boil. Boil gently, uncovered, until reduced slightly.

Remove most mussels from shells leaving a few for garnishing. Drain clams. Add mussels and clams to cooking juice. Sprinkle parsley over. Serve at once.

Serves 4.

CARBONARA SAUCE

30 g (1 oz/6 teaspoons) butter
8 rashers bacon, rinds removed, cut into matchsticks
4 eggs
60 g (2 oz/½ cup) grated Parmesan cheese
6 teaspoons single (light) cream
salt and pepper
3 teaspoons chopped fresh chives

In a saucepan, melt butter. Add bacon. Fry gently until cooked.

In a bowl, beat together eggs, Parmesan cheese and cream and season with salt and pepper. Pour onto bacon. Cook gently, stirring, until eggs are just beginning to thicken.

Stir in chives. Pour sauce over hot pasta, such as spaghetti or tagliatelle. Serve at once.

Serves 4.

SALMON & CREAM SAUCE

30 g (1 oz/6 teaspoons) butter
500 ml (16 fl oz/2 cups) double (thick) cream
30 g (1 oz/¼ cup) grated Parmesan cheese
250 g (8 oz/2 cups) cooked, flaked salmon
3 teaspoons chopped fresh dill
salt and pepper
pinch of freshly grated nutmeg
sprig of dill, to garnish

In a saucepan, heat butter and cream. Bring to just below boiling point.

Simmer gently for about 10 minutes, until thickened and slightly reduced. Add Parmesan cheese.

Stir in salmon, dill, salt, pepper and nutmeg. Serve, garnished with a sprig of dill, with spinach linguini or other thin noodles.

Serves 4 as a first course.

PESTO

60 g (2 oz) basil leaves
60 g (2 oz/½ cup) pine kernels
2 cloves garlic
salt
60 g (2 oz/½ cup) grated Parmesan cheese
125 ml (4 fl oz/½ cup) olive oil

Put basil, pine kernels, garlic and salt into a blender or food processor. Process until mixture forms a smooth paste.

Add grated Parmesan cheese to basil mixture in blender or food processor, then process until well blended.

Gradually add olive oil, a little at a time, until sauce has a creamy consistency.

Serves 4-6.

Note: Pesto is used as a sauce for pasta, and is also added to dishes such as minestrone soup to give added flavour.

Variation: When fresh basil is unavailable, a version of pesto may be made with parsley, and walnuts may be used instead of pine kernels.

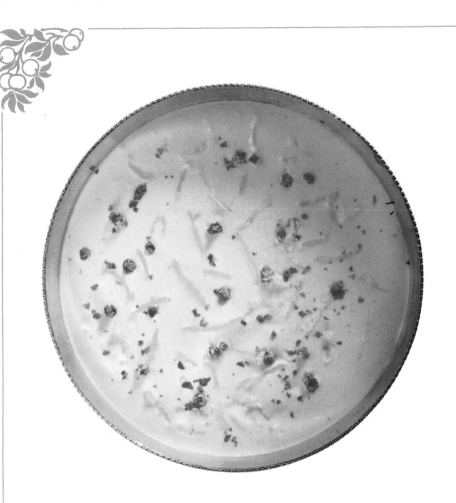

LEMON PEPPER SAUCE

30 g (1 oz/6 teaspoons) butter
155 ml (5 fl oz/⅔ cup) single (light) cream
1-2 teaspoons green peppercorns
grated peel of 1 lemon
salt

In a saucepan, melt butter. Stir in cream.

Lightly crush peppercorns with the back of a spoon. Add to cream. Stir in lemon peel and salt.

Heat gently, without boiling, until slightly thickened. Combine with cooked pasta and serve.

Serves 4.

Note: This sauce is ideal for serving with fine capellini.

TOMATO SAUCE

500 g (1 lb) tomatoes
4 teaspoons olive oil
1 onion, finely chopped
1 clove garlic, crushed
3 teaspoons tomato purée (paste)
½ teaspoon sugar
3 teaspoons chopped fresh basil
salt and pepper

Put tomatoes in a bowl. Pour over boiling water to cover. Leave for 1 minute. Drain. Peel and chop roughly.

In a saucepan, heat oil. Add onion and garlic. Cook until soft. Stir in chopped tomatoes, tomato purée (paste), sugar, basil, salt and pepper.

Cover pan, simmer gently for about 30 minutes. If a thicker sauce is required, simmer, uncovered, for a few more minutes. Serve with all types of pasta.

Serves 4.

MEATBALLS & SPAGHETTI

1 slice bread, crusts removed
1 onion, very finely chopped
1 clove garlic, crushed
500 g (1 lb) ground beef
3 teaspoons chopped fresh parsley
salt and pepper
3 teaspoons vegetable oil
1 quantity Tomato Sauce, see page 65
375 g (12 oz) spaghetti
60 g (2 oz/½ cup) grated parmesan cheese
sprigs of basil, to garnish

Soak bread in a little water. Squeeze dry and crumble into a bowl. Add onion, garlic, beef and parsley, salt and pepper. Mix well. Shape into 2.5 cm (1 in) balls. In a frying pan, heat oil. Add meatballs and cook for 10 minutes until brown all over. Add tomato sauce and heat through.

Meanwhile, cook spaghetti until tender. Drain well and pour into a heated serving dish. Pour over meatballs and sauce. Sprinkle with Parmesan cheese, garnish with sprigs of basil and serve.

Serves 4.

RICOTTA & HAM SAUCE

30 g (1 oz/6 teaspoons) butter
2 leeks, finely sliced
1 clove garlic, crushed
125g (4 oz) ham
250 g (8 oz/2 cups) Ricotta cheese
155 ml (5 fl oz/⅔ cup) thick sour cream
milk
pepper

In a saucepan, melt butter; add sliced leeks and garlic. Cook until leeks are soft.

Cut ham into small squares. Stir into leeks. Cook for a few minutes.

In a bowl, mix together Ricotta and sour cream. Add a little milk, if necessary, to make a smooth creamy sauce. Season with pepper. Add to pan with leeks and ham. Cook gently until sauce is heated through. Serve at once with tagliatelle.

Serves 4.

BÉCHAMEL SAUCE

315 ml (10 fl oz/1¼ cups) milk
½ bay leaf
60 g (2 oz/6 teaspoons) butter
60 g (2 oz/½ cup) plain flour
salt and pepper

In a small saucepan, heat the milk and bay leaf to just below boiling point. Remove from heat. Remove bay leaf.

In a heavy saucepan, melt butter. Stir in flour and cook for 2 minutes, stirring, over gentle heat. Remove from heat.

Gradually stir in milk. Return pan to heat. Stir until thick and smooth. Simmer gently for 10 minutes. Season with salt and pepper.

If sauce is not to be used immediately, cover surface closely with plastic wrap.

Serves 4.

Variation: For Ham & Mushroom Sauce, put 185g (6 oz) sliced mushrooms and 9 teaspoons dry cider into a saucepan, cover and cook gently for 5 minutes. Add to Béchamel Sauce made with 440 ml (14 fl oz/1¾ cups) milk and 45 g (1½ oz/9 teaspoons) each butter and plain flour. Stir in 125 g (4 oz) shredded ham and grated nutmeg to taste. Serve with pasta.

GREEN & BLUE SAUCE

250 g (8 oz) broccoli
185 g (6 oz) Gorgonzola cheese
100 g (3½ oz/½ cup) mascarpone
155 ml (5 fl oz/⅔ cup) natural yogurt
pepper

Wash and trim broccoli, discarding stalks. Cut into small flowerets. Cook in boiling salted water for 2-3 minutes until just tender. Drain thoroughly.

Roughly chop Gorgonzola cheese. In a small saucepan, put Gorgonzola and mascarpone. Heat gently, stirring, until Gorgonzola has melted.

Add broccoli and yogurt to cheese sauce. Season with pepper. Heat gently for 2 minutes, stirring occasionally. Pour over pasta.

Serves 4.

MEDITERRANEAN SAUCE

1 aubergine (eggplant)

salt

4 tablespoons olive oil

1 onion, chopped

1 clove garlic, crushed

1 small green pepper (capsicum), seeded

1 small red pepper (capsicum), seeded

1 small yellow pepper (capsicum), seeded

4 tomatoes, peeled and roughly chopped

salt and pepper

½ teaspoon dried oregano

Cut aubergine (eggplant) into strips, put into a colander and sprinkle with salt. Leave for 1 hour.

Pat aubergine slices dry with absorbent kitchen paper.

In a large frying pan, heat oil. Add onion and garlic. Cook gently until soft. Add aubergine (eggplant) strips. Cook for 5 minutes, stirring.

Cut peppers (capsicums) into strips, add to pan and cook for 5 minutes. Stir in tomatoes, salt, pepper and oregano. Cover pan and cook gently for 20 minutes. Serve with spaghetti.

Serves 4.

BOLOGNESE SAUCE

2 tablespoons vegetable oil

60 g (2 oz) rashers bacon, rinds removed, chopped

1 onion, finely chopped

1 carrot, finely chopped

1 stick celery, finely chopped

1 clove garlic, crushed

250 g (8 oz) ground beef

125 g (4 oz) chicken livers, chopped

6 teaspoons tomato purée (paste)

125 ml (4 fl oz/½ cup) dry white wine

125 ml (4 fl oz/½ cup) stock

salt and pepper

pinch of freshly grated nutmeg

celery leaves, to garnish

In a large heavy saucepan, heat oil. Add bacon and cook gently until fat begins to run from the bacon, stirring frequently.

Add onion, carrot, celery and garlic to pan. Cook, stirring, until beginning to brown. Add ground beef and cook, stirring, until evenly browned. Stir in chicken livers and cook for a few minutes, stirring frequently, until they are no longer pink.

Stir in tomato purée (paste), wine and stock and season with salt and pepper and nutmeg. Cover pan and cook gently for 30-40 minutes. Garnish with celery leaves and serve with spaghetti.

Serves 4-6.

CANNELLONI AU GRATIN

60 g (2 oz / ¼ cup) butter
1 onion, finely chopped
1 clove garlic, crushed
375 g (12 oz) mushrooms, sliced
3 teaspoons plain flour
185 ml (6 fl oz / ¾ cup) crème fraîche
salt and pepper
pinch of freshly grated nutmeg
1-egg quantity Herb Pasta, see page 51
6 very thin slices prosciutto
30 g (1 oz / ½ cup) fresh breadcrumbs
30 g (1 oz / ¼ cup) grated Parmesan cheese
slices of prosciutto and sprigs of mint,
to garnish

In a saucepan, melt the butter. Add onion and garlic and cook until soft. Add mushrooms and cook, stirring, until soft and most of the liquid has evaporated.

Stir in flour, then add 75 ml (2½ fl oz / ⅓ cup) crème fraîche to form a thick sauce. Season with salt, pepper and nutmeg.

Preheat oven to 180C (350F / Gas 4). Grease an ovenproof dish. Roll out pasta, see page 52, and cut 6 rectangles 12.5 × 10 cm (5 × 4 in). Put a slice of prosciutto on each rectangle, lay some mushroom filling across each one and roll up from the short end.

Pack tightly, seams down, in the dish. Pour remaining crème fraîche over and scatter with mixed breadcrumbs and Parmesan. Bake in oven for 20 minutes or until golden and bubbling. Serve at once, garnished with slices of prosciutto and sprigs of mint.

Serves 6 as a first course.

SPINACH CANNELLONI

500 g (1 lb) fresh spinach, trimmed
and washed
30 g (1 oz / 6 teaspoons) butter
1 onion, finely chopped
3 teaspoons plain flour
155 ml (5 fl oz / ⅔ cup) milk
125 g (4 oz / ½ cup) ham, finely chopped
salt and pepper
pinch of freshly grated nutmeg
8 ready-to-use cannelloni tubes
1 quantity Béchamel sauce, see page 67
90 g (3 oz / ¾ cup) grated Cheddar cheese
slices of ham and bay leaves, to
garnish

In a large saucepan, cook spinach in a little water until tender. Drain spinach and chop finely.

In a saucepan, melt butter, add onion and cook until soft. Stir in flour and cook for 1 minute. Gradually add milk and bring to the boil for 1 minute. Stir in spinach and ham. Season with salt, pepper and nutmeg. Push spinach mixture into cannelloni tubes using a teaspoon.

Preheat oven to 220C (425F / Gas 7). In a saucepan, gently heat white sauce. Stir in 60 g (2 oz / ½ cup) cheese. Pour half the sauce into an ovenproof dish. Arrange cannelloni in dish and pour over remaining sauce, arrange ham in a lattice pattern and sprinkle remaining cheese on top. Bake in the oven for 40 minutes until golden and bubbling. Serve, garnished with bay leaves.

Serves 4.

LOBSTER SHELLS

8 conchiglie (large shells)

meat from a 500 g (1 lb) cooked lobster

2 teaspoons lemon juice

salt

cayenne pepper

155 ml (5 fl oz/⅔ cup) double (heavy) cream

½ teaspoon grated lemon peel

2 teaspoons chopped fresh dill

pepper

lemon twist and sprigs of dill, to garnish

In a large saucepan of boiling salted water, cook shells, until just tender. Drain.

Preheat oven to 190C (375F/Gas 5). Chop lobster meat roughly. Put into a bowl with lemon juice, salt, cayenne pepper and 6 teaspoons cream. Mix well together. Fill shells with lobster mixture. Arrange in an ovenproof dish.

In a bowl, mix together remaining cream, lemon peel and dill. Season with salt and pepper. Pour over shells. Cover dish with foil. Bake in the oven for 15-20 minutes until heated through. Baste with sauce halfway through cooking time.

Garnish with a lemon twist and sprigs of dill. Serve at once.

Serves 4 as a first course.

FISH RAVIOLI

250 g (8 oz) white fish fillets, such as cod, cooked and flaked

2 canned anchovies, drained and pounded

30 g (1 oz/¼ cup) grated Parmesan cheese

grated peel and juice of ½ a lemon

1 egg yolk

pepper

freshly grated nutmeg

3-egg quantity Pasta Dough, see page 51

chopped fresh parsley, blanched shredded leek and strips of lemon peel, to garnish

LEEK SAUCE:

60 g (2 oz/¼ cup) butter

500 g (1 lb) leeks, cleaned and sliced

155 ml (5 fl oz/⅔ cup) fish or chicken stock

155 ml (5 fl oz/⅔ cup) thick sour cream.

In a bowl, mix the fish, anchovies, Parmesan cheese, lemon peel and juice and egg yolk. Season with pepper and nutmeg. Process in a blender or food processor until fairly smooth. Roll out pasta dough and, using fish purée as a filling, make ravioli, see page 54.

While ravioli is drying, make sauce. Melt butter in a saucepan, add leeks and stir round until coated with butter. Cover pan and cook gently until leeks are soft. Add stock, then process in a blender or food processor until smooth. Stir in sour cream. Cook ravioli in boiling water for 8-10 minutes. Meanwhile, warm sauce. Drain ravioli and turn into a warmed serving dish. Pour over sauce. Serve, garnished with parsley, leek and lemon peel.

Serves 6 as a first course.

PASTA & RICOTTA

500 g (1 lb) spinach, washed and trimmed
250 g (8 oz / 2 cups) Ricotta cheese
60 g (2 oz / ½ cup) grated Parmesan cheese
1 egg yolk
salt and pepper
freshly grated nutmeg
3-egg quantity Pasta Dough, see page 51
90 g (3 oz / ⅓ cup) butter
5 teaspoons chopped fresh mixed herbs
2 teaspoons lemon juice

In a large saucepan, cook spinach in a small amount of water until tender. Drain and leave to cool.

Squeeze spinach dry, then chop in a blender or food processor. Add Ricotta, Parmesan cheese and egg yolk and season with salt, pepper and nutmeg. Process until fairly smooth. Roll out the pasta, see page 12. Cut into 5 cm (2 in) squares. Put ½ teaspoon of filling in middle of each square. Fold in half to make a triangle; press edges to seal. Wrap long side of triangle around index finger; press ends together. Leave on a tea towel to dry, turning after 1 hour.

Cook pasta in a large pan of boiling water for 10-15 minutes. In a small saucepan, melt butter. Stir in herbs and lemon juice. Drain pasta and put into a warmed serving dish. Pour herb butter over and stir thoroughly. Serve at once.

Serves 4 as a main course or 6 as a first course.

Variation: If you have left over Pasta Verde or Tomato Pasta, see page 51, make a mixture of different coloured shapes. If preferred, cut pasta into 5 cm (2 in) circles instead of squares to make this dish.

RAVIOLI WITH SAGE

90 g (3 oz / ⅓ cup) butter
1 onion, peeled and chopped
250 g (8 oz) minced pork
250 g (8 oz) minced veal
2 tablespoons tomato purée (paste)
salt and pepper
freshly grated nutmeg
30 g (1 oz / ½ cup) breadcrumbs
2 egg yolks
125 g (4 oz / 1 cup) grated Parmesan cheese
3-egg quantity Pasta Dough, see page 51
fresh sage leaves

To make filling, in a saucepan, melt 30 g (1 oz/6 teaspoons) butter, add onion and cook until soft.

Add minced meats and cook, stirring, until brown. Blend tomato purée (paste) with 4 tablespoons water, then stir into pan. Season with salt, pepper and nutmeg to taste. Cover and cook gently for 30 minutes. Leave to cool, then put into a blender or food processor with the breadcrumbs, egg yolks and cheese and process until smooth. Make ravioli, see page 54, filling with meat mixture.

Drop ravioli in boiling salted water and cook for 10-15 minutes. Drain and place in a warmed serving dish. Melt remaining butter and pour over ravioli. Season with pepper and garnish with sage leaves. Serve at once.

Serves 6 as a first course.

TORTELLINI & TOMATO

315 g (10 oz) cooked chicken

125 g (4 oz / ½ cup) mortadella

2 eggs

60 g (2 oz / ½ cup) grated Parmesan
cheese

salt and pepper

freshly grated nutmeg

3-egg quantity Pasta Dough, see
page 51

1 quantity Tomato Sauce, see
page 65

Parmesan cheese for sprinkling

In a blender or food processor, finely chop chicken and mortadella. Add eggs and Parmesan cheese. Season with salt, pepper and nutmeg, then process until fairly smooth.

Roll out pasta, see page 52. Using a plain biscuit cutter, cut out rounds 4 cm (1½ in) in diameter. Put ½ teaspoon of filling in the middle of each round, see page 54.

Fold each round in half over the stuffing so that the upper edge comes just short of the lower edge. Press edges to seal. Curl round index finger, pressing the two points firmly together. Leave on a tea towel to dry, turning after 1 hour.

Cook tortellini in a large saucepan of boiling salted water for about 10 minutes. Meanwhile, in a saucepan, heat tomato sauce. Drain tortellini, tip into a warmed serving dish, pour sauce over, sprinkle with Parmesan cheese and serve.

Serves 4 as a main course or 6 as a first course.

VERMICELLI FLAN

30 g (1 oz/6 teaspoons) butter

2 small leeks, sliced

6 rashers bacon, rinds removed,
chopped

125 g (4 oz) fine vermicelli

60 g (2 oz/½ cup) grated Cheddar cheese

155 ml (5 fl oz/⅔ cup) natural yogurt

155 ml (5 fl oz/⅔ cup) single (light) cream

2 eggs, beaten

salt and pepper

1 tomato, sliced

leek leaves, to garnish

In a frying pan, heat butter. Add leeks and bacon. Cook gently until leeks are tender.

Preheat oven to 190C (375F/Gas 5). Grease a 22.5 cm (9 in) flan tin. Meanwhile, in a large saucepan of boiling salted water, cook vermicelli until tender. Drain, return to pan. Stir in cheese. Press vermicelli into the base and sides of flan tin.

Spread bacon and leeks over pasta flan case. In a bowl, beat together yogurt, cream, eggs, salt and pepper. Pour over bacon and leeks. Arrange tomato slices on top. Bake in the oven for 30 minutes or until puffed up and golden brown. Remove flan ring and serve warm or cold, garnished with leek leaves.

Serves 6.

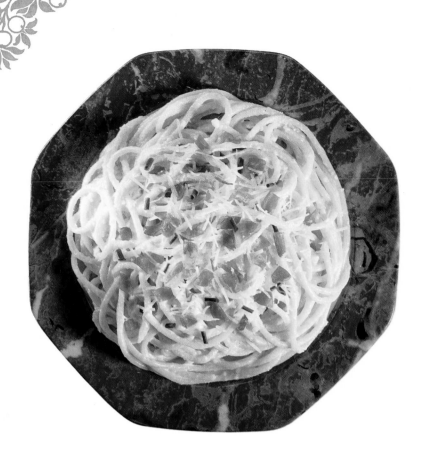

FOUR CHEESE BUCATINI

185 g (6 oz) bucatini
315 ml (10 fl oz/1¼ cups) single (light) cream
60 g (2 oz/½ cup) grated Parmesan cheese
90 g (3 oz) Gruyère cheese, diced
90 g (3 oz/¾ cup) soft goat's cheese
90 g (3 oz) Mozzarella cheese, diced
pepper
chopped Parma ham and chives, to garnish

In a large saucepan of boiling salted water, cook bucatini until tender.

Meanwhile, put cream into a large saucepan with half the Parmesan cheese. Add Gruyère, goat's cheese and Mozzarella. Heat gently until cheeses are melting. Season with pepper.

Drain bucatini. Add to cheese mixture. Stir well. Sprinkle with remaining Parmesan cheese, the Parma ham and chives. Serve at once.

Serves 4.

LASAGNE

250 g (8 oz) lasagne
1 quantity Béchamel Sauce, see page 67
125 g (4 oz) Mozzarella cheese, cubed
1 quantity Bolognese Sauce, see page 68
6 teaspoons grated Parmesan cheese

In a large saucepan of boiling salted water, cook lasagne, in two batches, for about 10 minutes until just tender. Drain thoroughly. Spread out on a tea towel.

Preheat the oven to 180C (350F/ Gas 4). Grease a rectangular oven-proof dish. In a saucepan, heat Béchamel sauce. Add Mozzarella cheese and stir until melted.

Arrange a layer of lasagne over base of dish. Spoon over half the meat sauce. Cover with lasagne. Spread with half the cheese sauce. Repeat the layers finishing with remaining cheese sauce. Sprinkle Parmesan cheese over top. Bake in the oven for 30-40 minutes.

Serves 4-6.

Note: This dish may be prepared in advance and baked when required. Serve with a salad.

SPINACH PASTA ROLL

3 teaspoons vegetable oil

1 onion, finely chopped

500 g (1 lb) frozen spinach, thawed and drained

125 g (4 oz / ⅔ cup) cottage cheese

125 g (4 oz / 1 cup) grated Parmesan cheese

1 egg yolk

salt and pepper

1 quantity Pasta Dough, see page 51

60 g (2 oz / ¼ cup) butter

sprigs of watercress, to garnish

In a frying pan, heat oil. Add onion and cook until soft. Add spinach and cook for 2 minutes, stirring frequently.

In a bowl, mix together cottage cheese, half the Parmesan cheese and egg yolk. Season with salt and pepper. Stir in spinach and onion. Roll out pasta dough to a rectangle 30 x 35 cm (12 × 14 in), joining two sheets of pasta together if necessary and moistening the seam with water. Spread with spinach mixture, leaving a border around edge.

Roll up from long edge. Cut in half to make 2 rolls.

Wrap each roll in greaseproof paper, then foil, leaving seam at top. Turn up end of foil to form 'handles'.

Put sufficient water in a pan to come halfway up rolls. Bring to boil, cover and simmer rolls for 30 minutes. Remove from pan, unwrap and leave to cool. Preheat oven to 190C (375F/Gas 5). Cut rolls into 2 cm (¾ in) slices. Arrange in baking dish. Melt butter and pour over slices. Sprinkle with remaining Parmesan. Bake in the oven for 15 minutes until golden. Serve, garnished with sprigs of watercress.

Serves 4.

FISH & PASTA RING

185 g (6 oz) tagliatelle verde

30 g (1 oz / 6 teaspoons) butter

4 eggs, beaten

315 ml (10 fl oz / 1¼ cups) milk

salt and pepper

freshly grated nutmeg

500 g (1 lb) white fish fillets, such as cod

1 quantity Tomato Sauce, see page 65

bay leaves, to garnish

In a large saucepan of boiling salted water, cook tagliatelle until tender. Meanwhile, preheat oven to 180C (350F/Gas 4).

In a small saucepan, melt butter. Brush a ring mould generously with melted butter. In a bowl, beat together eggs, milk and remaining butter. Season with salt, pepper and nutmeg. Pour mixture into ring mould. Drain tagliatelle, spoon into ring mould and arrange evenly. Bake in oven for 40 minutes until set.

Meanwhile, skin fish and cut into cubes. Put tomato sauce into a saucepan. Bring to the boil, then add fish. Simmer gently, uncovered, for 10-15 minutes, or until fish is cooked.

Turn out pasta ring onto a large warmed serving dish. Spoon some fish sauce into the centre, pour a little over top of pasta ring and arrange remaining fish and sauce round the edge. Garnish with bay leaves and serve at once.

Serves 4.

SMOKED FISH LASAGNE

500 g (1 lb) smoked fish fillets, such as haddock
625 ml (20 fl oz/2½ cups) milk
4 carrots, cut into small dice
4 sticks celery, cut into small dice
90 g (3 oz/⅓ cup) butter
6 sheets lasagne verde
3 teaspoons chopped fresh parsley
salt and pepper
60 g (2 oz/½ cup) plain flour
freshly grated nutmeg
30 g (1 oz/6 teaspoons) grated Parmesan cheese
lime twist and sprig of parsley, to garnish

Put fish and milk into a large saucepan. Bring to the boil, then simmer gently until fish is cooked.

Put carrots and celery into a saucepan with 30 g (1 oz/6 teaspoons) butter and 500 ml (16 fl oz/2 cups) water. Bring to the boil, then simmer until vegetables are tender. Meanwhile, in a large pan of boiling salted water, cook lasagne until just tender. Drain and spread out on a tea towel. Drain fish, reserving cooking liquid, and flake into a bowl. Drain vegetables, reserving liquid, and add to fish with parsley. Season with salt and pepper.

Preheat oven to 190C (375F/Gas 5). Make a Béchamel sauce, see page 67, with remaining butter, flour, vegetable water and milk from fish. Season with salt, pepper and nutmeg. Arrange a layer of lasagne in the base of an ovenproof dish. Cover with one-third of fish mixture then one-third of sauce. Repeat layers twice, ending with sauce. Sprinkle with Parmesan cheese. Bake in the oven for 25 minutes. Serve, garnished with lime twist and parsley.

Serves 4-6.

TUNA & MACARONI LAYER

185 g (6 oz/1¼ cups) wholewheat macaroni
90 g (3 oz/¾ cup) grated Cheddar cheese
220 g (7 oz) can tuna fish
½ quantity Béchamel Sauce, see page 67
2 teaspoons lemon juice
2 hard-boiled eggs, chopped
3 teaspoons chopped fresh parsley
salt and pepper
lemon slices and sprigs of parsley, to garnish

In a large saucepan of boiling salted water, cook macaroni until tender. Drain and mix with 60 g (2 oz/½ cup) cheese.

Meanwhile, drain tuna fish. Flake into a saucepan with Béchamel sauce, lemon juice, chopped eggs and parsley and season with salt and pepper. Mix gently together. Cook over a low heat until warmed through.

Divide tuna mixture between 4 individual flameproof bowls or casserole dishes. Top with macaroni and cheese. Sprinkle remaining cheese over the top. Brown under a medium grill until golden and bubbling. Serve, garnished with lemon slices cut into triangles and sprigs of parsley.

Serves 4.

KIDNEY & PASTA TURBIGO

| 4 lamb's kidneys |
| 60 g (2 oz/¼ cup) butter |
| 8 cocktail sausages |
| 125 g (4 oz) button mushrooms |
| 24 button onions, peeled |
| 1 teaspoon tomato purée (paste) |
| 2 teaspoons plain flour |
| 155 ml (5 fl oz/⅔ cup) beef stock |
| 3 teaspoons dry sherry |
| 1 bay leaf |
| salt and pepper |
| 185 g (6 oz/3 cups) pasta spirals |
| sprigs of thyme, to garnish |

Cut kidneys in half and remove core from each one.

In a saucepan, melt butter. Add kidneys and sausages. Cook, stirring occasionally, until brown. Remove from pan and set aside. Add mushrooms and onions to pan. Cook for 5-6 minutes, stirring occasionally.

Stir in tomato purée (paste) and flour. Cook for 1-2 minutes. Stir in stock and sherry. Bring to the boil. Return kidneys and sausages to pan with bay leaf. Season with salt and pepper. Cover pan and simmer for 20-25 minutes.

Meanwhile, in a large pan of boiling salted water, cook pasta until tender. Drain. Stir into kidney mixture. Serve, garnished with sprigs of thyme.

Serves 3-4.

COURGETTE PASTA BAKE

| 3 courgettes (zucchini), sliced |
| 375 g (12 oz/4 cups) rigatoni |
| 1 quantity Tomato Sauce, see page 65 |
| 250 g (8 oz) Mozzarella cheese, thinly sliced |
| 1 teaspoon olive oil |
| sprigs of basil, to garnish |

In a saucepan of boiling water, cook sliced courgettes (zucchini) for a few minutes until cooked but still firm. Drain and set aside.

Preheat oven to 180C (350F/Gas 4). Butter an ovenproof dish. Meanwhile, in a large pan of boiling salted water, cook rigatoni until almost tender. Drain and rinse in cold water. Place a third of the rigatoni in the dish.

Spread a third of the tomato sauce over the rigatoni, followed by a third of the Mozzarella cheese. Repeat layers; spread courgettes (zucchini) over Mozzarella.

Cover with remaining rigatoni, tomato sauce and Mozzarella. Sprinkle with olive oil. Bake in the oven for 20 minutes until Mozzarella cheese has melted over the top. Serve, garnished with basil.

Serves 4-6.

PORK & BEANS

6 teaspoons vegetable oil
375 g (12 oz) pork fillet, cut into thin slices
1 onion, chopped
1 clove garlic, crushed
185 g (6 oz / 1¼ cups) wholewheat pasta grills
440 g (14 oz / 1¾ cups) can cannellini beans
9 teaspoons chopped fresh parsley
9 teaspoons tomato purée (paste)
1 litre (32 fl oz / 4 cups) chicken stock
salt and pepper
chopped fresh parsley, to garnish

In a saucepan, heat oil. Add pork, in batches, and fry until browned.

Remove pork from pan and set aside. Add onion and garlic to pan and cook until beginning to soften. Return pork to pan, stir in pasta, drained beans, parsley, tomato purée (paste) and stock and season with salt and pepper.

Bring to the boil. Cover pan and simmer, stirring occasionally, for about 20 minutes, or until pasta is tender and most of the liquid absorbed. Add more stock if liquid is absorbed before pasta is cooked. Transfer to a warmed serving dish and garnish with chopped parsley. Serve at once.

Serves 4.

DEVILLED CRAB

60 g (2 oz / 1 cup) small pasta shells
250 g (8 oz / 1¾ cups) crabmeat
1 teaspoon Dijon mustard
2 teaspoons Worcestershire sauce
juice of ½ a lemon
125 ml (4 fl oz / ½ cup) natural yogurt
salt and cayenne pepper
6 teaspoons fresh breadcrumbs
30 g (1 oz / ¼ cup) grated Parmesan cheese
strips of lemon peel and whole fresh chives, to garnish

In a large saucepan of boiling salted water, cook pasta shells until tender. Drain.

In a bowl, combine crabmeat, mustard, Worcestershire sauce, lemon juice, yogurt and pasta. Season with salt and cayenne pepper.

Grease 6 scallop shells and divide mixture between them. In a bowl, mix together breadcrumbs and Parmesan cheese.

Sprinkle crumbs over crab mixture. Cook under a medium grill for about 10 minutes, or until golden. Serve at once, garnished with strips of lemon peel and whole chives.

Serves 6 as a first course.

FRANKFURTER BAKE

6 teaspoons vegetable oil
1 onion, sliced
2 sticks celery, sliced
6 frankfurters, cut into 2.5 cm (1 in) lengths
2 tomatoes, skinned and chopped
185 g (6 oz/3 cups) pasta wheels
2 teaspoons cornflour
155 ml (5 fl oz/⅔ cup) thick sour cream
1 tablespoon tomato purée (paste)
salt and pepper
sprigs of parsley and thick sour cream, to serve, if desired

In a large frying pan, heat oil. Add onion, celery and frankfurters. Cook, stirring occasionally, until onion and celery are soft. Add tomatoes and cook for a further 5 minutes.

Preheat oven to 220C (425F/Gas 7). Meanwhile, in a large pan of boiling salted water, cook pasta.

In a bowl, blend cornflour and a little sour cream. Stir in remaining cream. Add to vegetables in frying pan with tomato purée (paste). Season with salt and pepper.

Drain pasta wheels and stir into vegetable mixture. Pour into an ovenproof dish and bake in the oven for 10 minutes. Serve at once, garnished with sprigs of parsley and sour cream, if desired.

Serves 4.

VERMICELLI TIMBALLO

125 g (4 oz) fine vermicelli
½ quantity Béchamel Sauce, see page 67
30 g (1 oz/½ cup) fresh breadcrumbs
125 g (4 oz) Mozzarella cheese
125 g (4 oz) ham
sprigs of mint, to garnish
Tomato sauce, see page 65, to serve

In a large saucepan of boiling salted water, cook vermicelli until just tender. Drain. In a bowl, combine vermicelli and Béchamel sauce. Set aside.

Preheat oven to 220C (425F/Gas 7). Butter six 155 ml (5 fl oz/⅔ cup) moulds or ovenproof teacups. Coat with half the breadcrumbs.

Cut Mozzarella cheese and ham into small dice. Half fill each mould with pasta mixture. Divide Mozzarella and ham between moulds.

Fill moulds with remaining pasta mixture. Sprinkle the tops with remaining breadcrumbs.

Bake in the oven for 15 minutes. Run a sharp knife around inside of the moulds. Turn out onto warmed serving plates. Garnish each plate with a sprig of mint and serve with tomato sauce.

Serves 6.

BAKED COD ITALIENNE

30 g (1 oz / 6 teaspoons) butter

125 g (4 oz) mushrooms, sliced

1 quantity Tomato Sauce, see page 65

4 white fish steaks, such as cod

salt and pepper

125 g (4 oz / 2 cup) pasta shells

8 black olives and sprigs of watercress, to garnish

Preheat oven to 190C (375F/Gas 5). In a saucepan, melt butter. Add mushrooms and cook gently until soft. Stir in tomato sauce.

Put fish in a shallow ovenproof dish. Season with salt and pepper. Pour over tomato and mushroom sauce. Cover dish and bake in the oven for about 25 minutes, or until fish flakes when tested with a fork.

Meanwhile, cook pasta shells until just tender. Five minutes before the end of the baking time, arrange pasta round fish, spooning some of the sauce over it. Garnish with black olives and sprigs of watercress and serve.

Serves 4.

BROCCOLI PASTA SOUFFLÉ

250 g (8 oz) broccoli

125 g (4 oz/2 cups) pasta shells

45 g (1½ oz/9 teaspoons) butter

45 g (1½ oz/⅓ cup) plain flour

315 ml (10 fl oz/1¼ cups) milk

90 g (3 oz/¾ cup) grated Cheddar cheese

salt and pepper

freshly grated nutmeg

3 eggs, separated, plus 1 extra egg white

Divide broccoli into small flowerets. Cook in boiling salted water until just tender but still crisp. Drain.

In a large saucepan of boiling salted water, cook pasta shells until tender.

Preheat oven to 200C (400F/Gas 6). Grease a 1 litre (32 fl oz/4 cup) soufflé dish. In a saucepan, melt butter and stir in flour. Cook for 2 minutes, stirring over gentle heat. Gradually add milk and cook, stirring, until sauce thickens. Simmer gently for 5 minutes, then stir in grated cheese. Season with salt, pepper and nutmeg. Leave for a few minutes to cool slightly.

In a large bowl, whisk egg whites until stiff but not dry. Stir egg yolks into cheese sauce, then add broccoli and pasta. Stir 1 tablespoon of egg white into mixture, then gently fold in the rest. Pour mixture into soufflé dish. Bake in the oven for about 30 minutes until the soufflé is well risen, golden brown and just set in the middle. Serve at once.

Serves 4.

Note: This mixture may be cooked in individual soufflé dishes and baked for 20 minutes.

BOLOGNESE SOUFFLÉ

185 g (6 oz / 3 cups) wholewheat pasta spirals

1 quantity Bolognese Sauce, see page 68

3 eggs, separated

30 g (1 oz / ¼ cup) grated Parmesan cheese

Preheat oven to 190C (375F/Gas 5). Grease a 940 ml (30 fl oz/3¾ cup) soufflé dish. In a large saucepan of boiling salted water, cook pasta spirals until tender. Drain well. Stir into bolognese sauce.

Stir egg yolks into pasta mixture. In a bowl, beat egg whites until stiff but not dry. Stir 1 tablespoon of egg white into mixture, then gently fold in the rest.

Pour soufflé mixture into dish. Sprinkle with grated Parmesan cheese. Bake in the oven for 40 minutes, or until well risen and golden brown. Serve at once.

Serves 4.

Note: This mixture may be cooked in individual soufflé dishes and baked in the oven for 30 minutes.

PEPPER GRATIN

2 large red peppers (capsicums)

2 large yellow peppers (capsicums)

125 ml (4 fl oz/½ cup) olive oil

1 clove garlic, crushed

4 canned anchovies, drained and chopped

8 black olives, stoned and chopped

3 teaspoons capers

salt and pepper

250 g (8 oz) spaghetti

6 teaspoons fresh breadcrumbs

6 teaspoons Parmesan cheese, grated

strips of green pepper (capsicum) and black olives, to garnish

Cook peppers (capsicums) under a hot grill. Turn them at intervals until the skins are blistered and blackened.

Preheat the oven to 190C (375F/ Gas 5). Grease an ovenproof dish. Scrape skins off peppers (capsicums). Cut peppers (capsicums) into strips. In a frying pan, heat half oil. Add strips of pepper (capsicum) and garlic. Cook for 2-3 minutes until peppers (capsicums) soften. Stir in anchovies, olives and capers and season with salt and pepper.

Meanwhile, in a large saucepan of boiling salted water cook spaghetti until tender. Drain, return to pan; toss with half remaining olive oil. Combine breadcrumbs and Parmesan and sprinkle half over base of dish. Cover with half the pepper (capsicum) mixture, then with spaghetti. Cover with remaining pepper (capsicum) mixture. Sprinkle with remaining crumbs and cheese. Pour over remaining oil. Bake in the oven for 20 minutes, or until brown and crisp. Serve at once, garnished with strips of green pepper (capsicum) and black olives.

Serves 4.

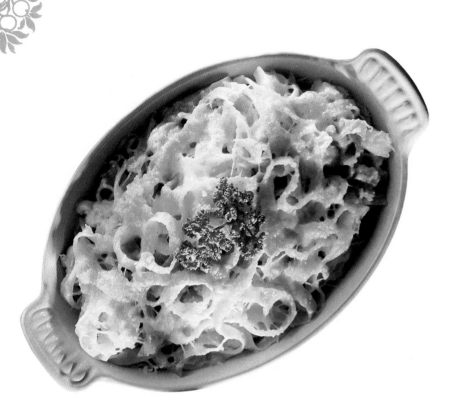

TURKEY TETRAZZINI

250 g (8 oz) red, green and white
tagliatelle
60 g (2 oz / ¼ cup) butter
4 rashers streaky bacon, rinds removed,
chopped
1 onion, finely chopped
125 g (4 oz) mushrooms, sliced
45 g (1½ oz / ⅓ cup) plain flour
440 ml (14 fl oz / 1¾ cups) chicken stock
155 ml (5 fl oz / ⅔ cup) double (thick)
cream
6 teaspoons dry sherry
375 g (12 oz) cooked turkey, cubed
salt and pepper
freshly grated nutmeg
30 g (1 oz / ¼ cup) grated Parmesan cheese
sprig of parsley, to garnish

Preheat oven to 180C (350F/Gas
4). In a large saucepan of boiling
salted water, cook tagliatelle until
tender. Drain.

In a saucepan, melt butter. Add
bacon and onion and cook until
onion is soft. Add the sliced mushrooms and cook until mushrooms
are just soft.

Stir in flour. Gradually stir in
stock, bring to boil and simmer,
stirring, until sauce is thickened and
smooth. Remove pan from the heat.
Stir in cream, sherry, turkey and
tagliatelle. Season with salt, pepper
and nutmeg. Pour into an ovenproof
dish. Sprinkle with Parmesan cheese.
Bake in the oven for 30 minutes, or
until the top is golden brown. Serve
at once, garnished with a sprig of
parsley.

Serves 4.

FISH & PASTA PIE

375 g (12 oz) smoked haddock
375 g (12 oz) fresh haddock
440 ml (14 fl oz / 1¾ cups) milk
185 g (6 oz / 1¼ cups) macaroni
30 g (1 oz / 6 teaspoons) butter
30 g (1 oz / ¼ cup) plain flour
1 teaspoon lemon juice
3 hard-boiled eggs, sliced
3 teaspoons chopped fresh parsley
salt and pepper
250 ml (8 fl oz / 1 cup) Greek strained
yogurt
2 eggs, beaten
90 g (3 oz / ¾ cup) grated Cheddar cheese
lemon slices and sprigs of parsley, to
garnish

Put fresh and smoked haddock in a
saucepan with milk and 315 ml (10
fl oz / 1¼ cups) water. Poach fish for
5-10 minutes until flesh flakes when
tested with a fork.

In a large saucepan of boiling
salted water, cook macaroni until
tender.

Preheat oven to 190C (375F/Gas
5). In a heavy saucepan, melt butter.
Stir in flour and cook for 2 minutes,
stirring over gentle heat. Remove
from heat and stir in 315 ml (10 fl
oz / 1¼ cups) of cooking liquid.
Return to heat and stir until thick
and smooth. Add lemon juice, hard-
boiled eggs, and parsley. Season with
salt and pepper. Pour mixture into
an ovenproof dish.

In a bowl, mix together yogurt
and beaten eggs. Stir in macaroni
and 60 g (2 oz / ½ cup) cheese. Pour
over fish mixture. Sprinkle with
remaining cheese. Bake in the oven
for 25-30 minutes until golden
brown. Serve, garnished with lemon
slices and sprigs of parsley.

Serves 4-6.

STUFFED PEPPERS

60 g (2 oz / 1 cup) pasta spirals
½ quantity Tomato Sauce, see page 65
2 teaspoons capers
6 black olives, stoned and chopped
2 red peppers (capsicums)
2 yellow peppers (capsicums)
2 teaspoons olive oil
sprig of basil, to garnish

Preheat oven to 190C (375F/Gas 5). Grease an ovenproof dish. In a large saucepan of boiling salted water, cook pasta spirals until tender. Drain.

In a bowl, mix together pasta, tomato sauce, capers and olives.

Slice off the stalk end of peppers (capsicums). Remove core and seeds. Fill peppers (capsicums) with pasta and tomato mixture. Replace tops of peppers (capsicums).

Stand peppers (capsicums) in the ovenproof dish. Pour a little olive oil over each one. Cook in oven for about 30 minutes, or until peppers (capsicums) are tender. Serve, garnished with a sprig of basil.

Serves 4.

— BEEF & MACARONI STRUDEL —

90 g (3 oz/⅓ cup) butter
30 g (1 oz/¼ cup) plain flour
185 ml (6 fl oz/¾ cup) milk
salt and pepper
125 g (4 oz/1 cup) macaroni
6 teaspoons vegetable oil
1 onion, finely chopped
250 g (8 oz) ground beef
3 teaspoons tomato purée (paste)
½ teaspoon ground cinnamon
3 teaspoons chopped fresh parsley
4 sheets filo pastry
tomato slices, onion rings and sprigs of parsley, to garnish

In a saucepan, make a Béchamel sauce, see page 67, with 30 g (1 oz/6 teaspoons) butter, the flour and milk. Season with salt and pepper.
In a large saucepan of boiling salted water, cook macaroni. Preheat oven to 190C (375F/Gas 5). Meanwhile, in a frying pan, heat oil. Add onion and cook until soft. Add ground beef and stir until well browned. Stir in tomato purée (paste), cinnamon and parsley. Season. Drain macaroni, then stir into beef mixture with sauce.

In a small saucepan, melt remaining butter. Brush a sheet of filo pastry with butter. Lay another sheet of pastry on top. Brush with more butter. Repeat with remaining pastry. Place macaroni mixture in a line along one long edge of pastry, leaving a space at each end. Tuck ends over, then roll up firmly.

Place on a baking sheet. Brush roll with butter. Bake in the oven for 45 minutes, or until brown and crisp, brushing with butter occasionally. Garnish and serve.

Serves 4.

Variation: Make individual strudels and bake for 20–25 minutes.

SPICY NOODLES

6 teaspoons vegetable oil

1 clove garlic, crushed

1 cm (½ in) piece fresh root ginger, peeled and grated

250 g (8 oz) spinach, roughly chopped

250 g (8 oz) white cabbage, shredded

315 ml (10 fl oz / 1¼ cups) chicken stock

3 teaspoons soy sauce

1 teaspoon chilli sauce

125 g (4 oz) fine egg noodles

In a wok or large frying pan, heat oil. Add garlic and ginger. Cook, stirring, for 1 minute.

Add spinach and cabbage. Cook, stirring, until they are bright green and almost tender. Stir in stock, soy sauce and chilli sauce.

Stir in noodles and simmer for a few minutes until tender. Serve as an accompaniment.

Serves 4.

SPICY SESAME NOODLES

6 teaspoons sesame seeds

3 teaspoons sesame oil

4 teaspoons peanut butter

2 tablespoons soy sauce

2 teaspoons chilli sauce

½ teaspoon sugar

250 g (8 oz) rice vermicelli

carrot flowers and toasted sesame seeds, to garnish

In a dry frying pan, cook sesame seeds over a medium heat until golden brown. Crush slightly.

In a bowl, or food processor, mix together sesame seeds, sesame oil, peanut butter, soy sauce, chilli sauce, sugar and 60 ml (2 fl oz/¼ cup) water. Set aside.

Put rice vermicelli into a bowl. Pour over enough boiling water to cover. Leave to soak for 10 minutes, then drain thoroughly. Put drained vermicelli and sesame sauce into a saucepan. Mix together to coat vermicelli in sauce. Cook over a low heat until mixture is thoroughly heated through. Serve, garnished with carrot flowers and sesame seeds.

Serves 4.

SINGAPORE NOODLES

6 teaspoons vegetable oil
125 g (4 oz) mushrooms, sliced
1 onion, finely chopped
1 clove garlic, crushed
125 g (4 oz) ham, cut into shreds
2.5 cm (1 in) piece fresh root ginger, peeled and grated
50 g (2 oz / ½ cup) frozen peas
250 g (8 oz) rice vermicelli
125 g (4 oz) cooked chicken
1 teaspoon curry powder
salt
125 g (4 oz) peeled prawns
75 ml (2½ fl oz / ⅓ cup) chicken stock
4 teaspoons soy sauce
60 ml (2 fl oz / ¼ cup) dry sherry
spring onion tassels, to garnish

In a large frying pan, heat vegetable oil. Add mushrooms, onion, garlic, ham and ginger. Stir well. Cook over a low heat for 10 minutes. Add peas and cook for 5 minutes.

Put rice vermicelli in a bowl. Pour boiling water over, to cover. Leave to soak for 10 minutes. Drain thoroughly. Meanwhile, cut the chicken into matchstick pieces. Stir curry powder and salt into mushroom and ham mixture.

Add chicken, prawns, stock, soy sauce and sherry; stir thoroughly. Add noodles and heat gently. Garnish with spring onion tassels.

Serves 4.

NOODLES WITH EGGS

375 g (12 oz) buckwheat noodles
2 tablespoons vegetable oil
1 onion, chopped
185 g (6 oz) Chinese leaves, shredded
4 eggs, beaten
3 teaspoons soy sauce
salt and pepper
bay leaf and lemon peel rose, to garnish

In a large saucepan of boiling salted water, cook buckwheat noodles in the same way as spaghetti, until just tender.

Meanwhile, in a heavy saucepan, heat oil. Add onion and cook until soft. Add Chinese leaves and cook until beginning to soften, then stir in beaten eggs. Cook, stirring, for about 1 minute until eggs are beginning to set.

Drain noodles and stir into egg mixture. Add soy sauce and season with salt and pepper. Serve at once, garnished with a bay leaf and lemon peel rose.

Serves 4.

— VERMICELLI & CHICK PEAS —

125 g (4 oz/⅔ cup) chick peas, soaked overnight
60 g (2 oz/¼ cup) butter
1 onion, finely chopped
185 g (6 oz) vermicelli
250 g (8 oz/1¾ cups) long grain rice
salt
75 ml (2½ fl oz/⅓ cup) thick sour cream
sprig of parsley, to garnish

Drain chick peas and rinse in cold water. Put chick peas and 750 ml (24 fl oz/3 cups) water into a saucepan. Bring to boil, then cover pan and simmer for 30 minutes, or until chick peas are tender.

In a large saucepan, melt butter. Add onion and cook gently until tender. Break vermicelli into 2.5 cm (1 in) pieces and add to pan. Stir until well coated with butter. Add rice and cook, stirring, until grains are transparent. Add 625 ml (20 fl oz/2½ cups) water and salt to taste. Bring to boil, then cover pan tightly and simmer for about 25 minutes, or until water is absorbed and rice is tender. Add more water if it dries up before rice is cooked.

Stir chick peas into vermicelli and rice. Cook over a low heat until heated through. Pour sour cream over the top and serve, garnished with a sprig of parsley.

Serves 6.

— SPAGHETTI LAYER —

2 aubergines (eggplants), sliced
salt
500 g (1 lb) spaghetti
olive oil
1 quantity Tomato Sauce, see page 65
3 hard-boiled eggs, thinly sliced
90 g (3 oz/¾ cup) grated Parmesan cheese
chopped hard-boiled egg, to garnish

Put the sliced aubergines (eggplants) into a colander. Sprinkle with salt and leave to drain for at least 30 minutes.

In a large saucepan of boiling salted water, cook spaghetti until tender. Drain.

Preheat oven to 190C (375F/Gas 5). Grease an ovenproof dish. Remove aubergine (eggplant) slices from colander and pat dry. In a frying pan, heat 2 tablespoons olive oil. Fry aubergine (eggplant) slices in batches until very tender, adding more oil as necessary. Drain on absorbent kitchen paper.

In a bowl, mix together spaghetti and tomato sauce. Spread one-third of spaghetti mixture in the ovenproof dish. Cover with half the aubergine (eggplant) slices and half the hard-boiled egg slices. Sprinkle with one-third of the Parmesan cheese. Repeat layers then finish with a layer of spaghetti. Sprinkle with remaining Parmesan. Bake in the oven for 30 minutes until golden. Serve, garnished with chopped hard-boiled egg.

Serves 6.

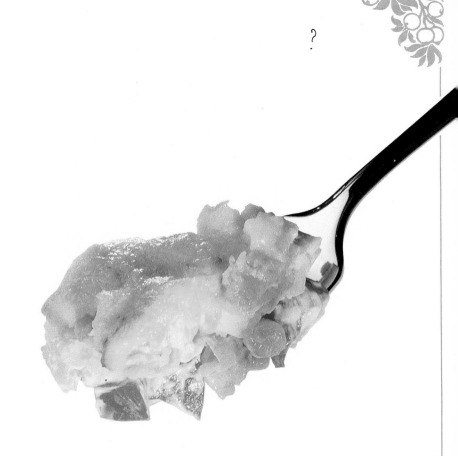

VEGETABLE CASSEROLE

2 tablespoons vegetable oil	
1 onion, finely sliced	
2 teaspoons plain flour	
1 tablespoon paprika	
440 g (14 oz) can tomatoes	
250 g (8 oz) cauliflower flowerets	
2 carrots, roughly chopped	
½ green pepper (capsicum), seeded and roughly chopped	
2 courgettes (zucchini), roughly chopped	
125 g (4 oz/2 cups) wholewheat pasta shells	
salt and pepper	
155 ml (5 fl oz/⅔ cup) Greek strained yogurt	
sprig of parsley, to garnish	

In a saucepan, heat oil. Add onion and cook until soft.

Stir in flour and paprika. Cook, stirring, for 1 minute. Add tomatoes and 315 ml (10 fl oz/1¼ cups) water. Bring to the boil, then stir in cauliflower, carrots, green pepper (capsicum), courgettes (zucchini) and pasta. Season with salt and pepper. Cover pan and simmer for 40 minutes, or until pasta is tender.

Gently stir yogurt into vegetable mixture and serve, garnished with a sprig of parsley.

Serves 4.

MACARONI BAKE

125 g (4 oz) leeks, thinly sliced	
125 g (4 oz/¾ cup) wholewheat macaroni	
2 sticks celery	
1 red pepper (capsicum)	
155 ml (5 fl oz/⅔ cup) natural yogurt	
125 g (4 oz/) low fat soft cheese	
2 teaspoons naturally fermented shoyu (soy sauce)	
salt and pepper	
60 g (2 oz/½ cup) grated Cheddar cheese	

Preheat oven to 180C (350F/Gas 4). Put leeks into a saucepan of boiling water. Bring back to the boil. Drain.

In a large saucepan of boiling salted water, cook macaroni until tender. Drain.

Finely chop celery and red pepper (capsicum). In a bowl, mix together leeks, celery, red pepper (capsicum) and macaroni.

In a bowl, mix together yogurt, low fat soft cheese and shoyu. Season with salt and pepper. Pour over macaroni mixture. Mix together thoroughly. Put into an ovenproof dish and sprinkle grated cheese over top. Bake in the oven for 30 minutes until golden and bubbling.

Serves 4.

VEGETARIAN BOLOGNESE

185 g (6 oz/1 cup) brown lentils
125 g (4 oz/⅔ cup) split peas
2 tablespoons vegetable oil
1 onion, finely chopped
1 clove garlic, crushed
1 carrot, finely chopped
1 stick celery, finely chopped
440 g (14 oz) can tomatoes
1 teaspoon dried oregano
salt and pepper
Parmesan cheese, to serve
sprig of parsley, to garnish

In a saucepan, bring 625 ml (20 fl oz/2½ cups) water to the boil. Stir in lentils and split peas. Simmer, covered, for about 40 minutes, or until all liquid has been absorbed and lentils and peas are soft.

In a saucepan, heat oil. Add onion, garlic, carrot and celery. Cook over a low heat, stirring occasionally, until soft. Stir in chopped tomatoes and oregano. Season with salt and pepper. Cover pan and simmer gently for 5 minutes.

Add lentils and split peas to pan. Cook, stirring, until well combined and heated through. Serve with wholewheat spaghetti sprinkled with Parmesan cheese and garnished with parsley.

Serves 4-6.

PASTA & VEGETABLE LOAF

125 g (4 oz/⅔ cup) brown lentils
125 g (4 oz/⅔ cup) split peas
125 g (4 oz/2 cups) small wholewheat pasta shapes
125 g (4 oz/½ cup) butter
1 onion, chopped
1 clove garlic, crushed
1 large carrot, scrubbed and chopped
1 stick celery, chopped
1 egg, beaten
½ teaspoon ground cumin
2 tablespoons chopped fresh parsley
salt and pepper
sprig of mint, to garnish

In a saucepan, bring 625 ml (20 fl oz/2½ cups) water to the boil. Stir in lentils and split peas. Simmer, covered, for about 40 minutes, or until all liquid has been absorbed and lentils and peas are soft.

Meanwhile, preheat oven to 190C (375F/Gas 5). Grease a 500 g (1 lb) loaf tin. In a large saucepan of boiling salted water, cook pasta shapes until tender.

In a saucepan, heat butter. Add onion, garlic, carrot and celery. Cook, stirring occasionally, until soft. Add lentils, split peas, pasta, beaten egg, cumin and parsley. Season with salt and pepper.

Mix together thoroughly. Spoon mixture into the loaf tin. Cover with foil. Bake in the oven for 40 minutes. Leave in tin for 5 minutes, then run a knife round edge of loaf and turn out onto a serving dish. Serve sliced, garnished with mint.

Serves 4.

Note: This loaf may be served hot with tomato sauce or cold with salad.

VEGETARIAN LASAGNE

185 g (6 oz / 1 cup) aduki beans, soaked overnight

6-8 sheets wholewheat lasagne

2 tablespoons vegetable oil

1 onion, finely chopped

1 clove garlic, crushed

250 g (8 oz) white cabbage, shredded

125 g (4 oz) mushrooms, sliced

1 leek, roughly chopped

½ green pepper (capsicum), chopped

440 g (14 oz) can tomatoes

1 teaspoon dried oregano

salt and pepper

1 quantity Béchamel Sauce, see page 67, made with wholewheat flour

60 g (2 oz / ½ cup) grated Cheddar cheese

sprigs of watercress, to garnish

Drain aduki beans. Put into a saucepan with 1 litre (32 fl oz/4 cups) water. Bring to boil, cover pan and cook for 40 minutes.

In a large saucepan of boiling salted water, cook lasagne until tender. Drain and pat dry. In a saucepan, heat oil. Add onion and garlic and cook until soft. Stir in cabbage, mushrooms, leek, and pepper (capsicum) and cook for 5 minutes, stirring occasionally. Drain aduki beans, reserving cooking water, and add to vegetables.

Stir in tomatoes and 185 ml (6 fl oz/1 cup) cooking water from beans. Add oregano and season with salt and pepper. Cover pan and simmer gently for 30 minutes, stirring occasionally.

Preheat oven to 180C (350F/Gas 4). In an ovenproof baking dish, make layers of lasagne, vegetables and sauce, ending with a layer of sauce. Sprinkle grated cheese over top. Bake in the oven for 30 minutes until golden. Serve, garnished with watercress, with salad.

Serves 4-6.

PASTA PAN FRY

250 g (8 oz/4 cups) pasta bows

2 tablespoons vegetable oil

1 onion, chopped

1 green pepper (capsicum), seeded and chopped

125 g (4 oz) mushrooms, sliced

250 g (8 oz) chicken livers, chopped

250 g (8 oz) tomatoes, peeled and chopped

2 fresh sage leaves, chopped

salt and pepper

sage leaves, to garnish

In a large saucepan of boiling salted water, cook pasta bows until tender. Drain.

In a large frying pan, heat the oil.

Add onion and cook for a few minutes until soft.

Add green pepper (capsicum) and cook, stirring, for 3 minutes. Add mushrooms and cook, stirring, for a further 2 minutes. Add chicken livers and stir-fry until livers are no longer pink.

Stir tomatoes and sage into chicken liver mixture and season with salt and pepper. Cook, stirring, until the juice begins to run from tomatoes. Add pasta bows and heat. Serve, garnished with sage leaves.

Serves 3-4.

GOLDEN FRITTERS

60g (2 oz/½ cup) macaroni
2 eggs
125 g (4 oz/1 cup) grated Cheddar cheese
60 g (2 oz/⅔ cup) canned sweetcorn, drained
salt and pepper
vegetable oil for frying
sprigs of parsley, to garnish

In a large saucepan of boiling salted water, cook macaroni until tender. Drain and rinse thoroughly with cold water.

In a bowl, beat eggs, add macaroni, cheese and sweetcorn. Season to taste with salt and pepper and stir thoroughly.

In a frying pan, heat oil. Drop in tablespoons of macaroni mixture. Fry until each fritter is crisp and golden on the underside and the upper side is set. Turn and fry until the other side is crisp and golden. Drain on absorbent kitchen paper and serve garnished with parsley.

Serves 4.

DEEP-FRIED RAVIOLI

250 g (8 oz) frozen chopped spinach, cooked and drained
250 g (8 oz) cooked chicken
2 egg yolks
60 g (2 oz/½ cup) grated Parmesan cheese
salt and pepper
freshly grated nutmeg
3-egg quantity Pasta Dough, see page 51
vegetable oil for deep frying
lime and lemon slices and sprigs of parsley, to garnish

Squeeze as much water as possible from spinach. In a blender or food processor, process chicken, spinach, egg yolks, Parmesan cheese, salt, pepper and nutmeg until quite smooth.

Roll out pasta dough. Using chicken mixture as a filling, make ravioli, see page 54.

In a deep fat fryer, heat oil to 190C (375F) or until a cube of day-old bread browns in 40 seconds. Fry ravioli, in batches, until crisp and golden brown. Drain on absorbent kitchen paper and keep hot until all the ravioli are cooked. Serve at once, garnished with lime and lemon slices and sprigs of parsley.

Serves 4.

PIZZA-STYLE SPAGHETTINI

250 g (8 oz) spaghettini
125 g (4 oz/1 cup) grated Cheddar cheese
2 eggs, beaten
125 g (4 oz) salami, diced
½ teaspoon dried oregano
salt and pepper
vegetable oil for frying
2 tomatoes, sliced
6 black olives
sprigs of oregano, to garnish

In a large saucepan of boiling salted water, cook spaghettini until tender. Drain and rinse with cold water.

In a bowl, using hands, mix spaghettini, cheese, eggs, salami, and oregano thoroughly together. Season with salt and pepper.

In a frying pan, heat oil. Tip spaghettini mixture into pan and pat out evenly. Cook for about 5 minutes until the underside is brown and crisp, and the top is set.

Turn over onto a plate, then slide back into pan. Cook second side until brown and crisp. Turn onto a large serving plate and arrange tomato slices and olives on top. Garnish with sprigs of oregano.

Serves 4-6.

CRISPY CANNELLONI

8 cannelloni tubes
2 tablespoons vegetable oil
1 leek, finely chopped
250 g (8 oz) low fat soft cheese
125 g (4 oz) mortadella, chopped
1 teaspoon tomato purée (paste)
2 eggs
1 tablespoon chopped fresh parsley
salt and pepper
5 tablespoons fresh breadcrumbs
5 tablespoons grated Parmesan cheese
vegetable oil for deep frying
lemon slices and sprigs of parsley, to garnish

In a large saucepan of salted water, cook cannelloni for 4-5 minutes until almost soft. Drain cannelloni, rinse with cold water and spread out on a tea towel.

In a frying pan, heat oil. Fry chopped leek until soft. In a bowl, mix together leek, soft cheese, mortadella, tomato purée (paste), 1 egg and parsley. Season with salt and pepper.

Using a small teaspoon, push filling into cannelloni. Mix together breadcrumbs and Parmesan cheese. Spread out on a large plate. Beat remaining egg in a shallow dish. Roll cannelloni in beaten egg and coat with breadcrumb mixture.

In a deep fat fryer, heat oil to 190C (375F) or until a cube of day-old bread browns in 40 seconds. Fry cannelloni, 4 at a time, for 2-3 minutes until crisp and golden. Drain on absorbent kitchen paper. Keep hot until all the cannelloni are cooked. Serve, garnished with lemon slices and parsley.

Serves 4.

CRISPY NOODLES

185 g (6 oz/1⅔ cups) short cut noodles
1 large Spanish onion, thinly sliced
155 ml (5 fl oz/⅔ cup) milk
2 tablespoons plain flour
vegetable oil for deep frying
salt
spring onion tassels and lemon butterflies, to garnish

In a large saucepan of boiling salted water, cook the noodles until just tender. Drain, rinse in cold water, then drain again thoroughly.

In a deep fat fryer, heat oil to 190C (375F) or until a cube of day-old bread browns in 40 seconds. Fry noodles in 4 batches until crisp and golden. Drain on absorbent kitchen paper. Keep hot.

Separate onion slices into rings. Dip onion rings in milk, then toss in flour. Fry in 2 batches, in the same way as noodles, until crisp and golden. Mix with noodles and sprinkle with salt. Serve, with each portion garnished with a spring onion tassel and lemon butterfly.

Serves 4 as an accompaniment to fried or grilled meat or fish.

NOODLE PANCAKES

30 g (1 oz) noodles
60 g (2 oz) ham
2 eggs, beaten
1 tablespoon chopped fresh parsley
1 tablespoon grated Parmesan cheese
salt and pepper
vegetable oil for frying
lemon slices and sprigs of parsley, to garnish

In a large saucepan of boiling salted water, cook the noodles until just tender. Drain. Chop noodles and ham. In a bowl, mix with eggs, parsley and Parmesan cheese. Season to taste with salt and pepper.

In a frying pan, heat oil. Drop tablespoons of noodle mixture into pan. Cook until underside is crisp and brown, then turn over and fry other side.

Remove from pan. Drain on absorbent kitchen paper. Serve at once, garnished with lemon slices and sprigs of parsley.

Serves 4.

CHOCOLATE & NUT BOWS

30 g (1 oz/¼ cup) blanched almonds
30 g (1 oz/¼ cup) hazelnuts
250 g (8 oz/4 cups) pasta bows
30 g (1 oz/6 teaspoons) butter
60 g (2 oz/½ cup) plain (dark) chocolate, coarsely chopped
30 g (1 oz/6 teaspoons) demerara sugar

Put nuts in a grill pan under a medium grill. Cook, stirring frequently, until golden brown. Chop nuts coarsely.

In a large saucepan of boiling salted water, cook pasta bows until tender.

Drain pasta and put into a warmed serving dish. Stir in butter. Add nuts, chocolate and demerara sugar. Toss to mix. Serve at once.

Serves 4.

Variations: Use pasta butterflies instead of bows, if preferred.

ALMOND RAVIOLI

125 g (4 oz/1¼ cups) ground almonds
125 g (4 oz/½ cup) caster sugar
2 egg yolks
30 g (1 oz/6 teaspoons) butter
1 quantity Pasta Dough, see page 51
Greek style yogurt and raspberry leaves, to decorate
RASPBERRY SAUCE:
500 g (1 lb) raspberries
125 g (4 oz/½ cup) caster sugar

To make sauce, reserve a few raspberries for decoration and put raspberries and sugar into a saucepan. Heat gently until juice begins to run. Press through a sieve and set aside.

In a bowl, mix together ground almonds, sugar and egg yolks. In a small saucepan, melt butter. Add to almond mixture. Roll out pasta dough, see page 52. Make ravioli, see page 54, filling with the ground almond paste.

In a large saucepan of boiling salted water, cook ravioli for about 10 minutes. Drain. Meanwhile, in a saucepan, heat raspberry sauce. Pour a pool of sauce onto each plate and arrange ravioli on top. Pipe a circle of yogurt around dish then, using a skewer make a web effect. Decorate with reserved raspberries and raspberry leaves.

Serves 4.

APPLE LASAGNE

875 g (1¾ lb) cooking apples
30 g (1 oz/6 teaspoons) butter
60 g (2 oz/¼ cup) caster sugar
30 g (1 oz/¼ cup) raisins
¼ teaspoon mixed spice
6 sheets lasagne
30 g (1 oz/¼ cup) finely chopped walnuts
whipped cream, to serve
CUSTARD:
315 ml (10 fl oz/1¼ cups) milk
1 egg, plus 1 egg yolk
3 teaspoons cornflour
3 teaspoons caster sugar
icing sugar for sprinkling

To make custard, in a saucepan, heat milk. In a bowl, mix together egg, egg yolk, cornflour and sugar. Pour hot milk onto egg mixture.

Stir, return to saucepan and heat gently until thickened. Set aside.

Peel, core and slice apples. Put in a saucepan with butter, sugar and a little water. Cook for 10 minutes, or until soft. Stir in raisins and mixed spice.

Preheat oven to 190C (375F/Gas 5). Butter an ovenproof dish.

Meanwhile, in a large pan of boiling water, cook lasagne. Drain. Layer lasagne and apple mixture in the dish, ending with a layer of apple. Pour custard over apple. Sprinkle with walnuts. Bake in oven for 25 minutes. Sprinkle with icing sugar and serve with cream.

Serves 4.

APRICOT WALNUT LAYER

125 g (4 oz/1 cup) dried apricots, soaked overnight
2.5 cm (1 in) piece of cinnamon stick
juice and finely grated peel 1 orange
90 g (3 oz/½ cup) brown sugar
2 teaspoons arrowroot
30 g (1 oz/½ cup) fine fresh breadcrumbs
125 g (4 oz) tagliatelle
60 g (2 oz/½ cup) ground walnuts
30 g (1 oz/6 teaspoons) butter
walnut halves and apricot pieces, to decorate
whipped cream flavoured with grated orange peel, to serve

Drain apricots, reserving juice. Put apricots, 6 teaspoons of juice, cinnamon, orange juice and peel and 30 g (1 oz/2 tablespoons) sugar into a saucepan. Bring to the boil, then cover and simmer for 10-15 minutes until tender.

Blend arrowroot with a little water. Add to apricots. Cook gently, stirring, until mixture has thickened. Leave to cool.

Preheat oven to 190C (375F/Gas 5). Butter a soufflé dish, then coat with breadcrumbs.

Meanwhile, in a large saucepan of boiling salted water, cook tagliatelle until tender. Drain.

Put one-third of the pasta in dish. Cover with apricot mixture. Cover with half remaining pasta. Mix walnuts and remaining sugar together, spread over pasta. Top with final layer of pasta.

In a saucepan, melt butter. Pour over pasta. Bake in the oven for 25 minutes. Turn out onto a serving dish. Decorate with walnut halves and apricot pieces and serve with flavoured cream.

Serves 4-6.

DATE & NOODLE PUDDING

250 g (8 oz) tagliatelle
155 ml (5 fl oz/⅔ cup) Greek strained yogurt
125 g (4 oz/½ cup) mascarpone
1 teaspoon cornflour
3 eggs, beaten
6 teaspoons clear honey
1 teaspoon ground cinnamon
60 g (2 oz/⅓ cup) chopped dates
60 g (2 oz/⅓ cup) sultanas
60 g (2 oz/⅓ cup) glacé cherries, chopped
whipped cream, glacé cherries and strips of angelica, to decorate

In a large saucepan of boiling salted water, cook tagliatelle until tender. Drain.

Preheat oven to 180C (350F/Gas 4). Grease a rectangular ovenproof dish. In a bowl, mix yogurt and mascarpone. Stir in cornflour, eggs, honey, cinnamon, dates, sultanas and cherries.

Add tagliatelle and stir well to distribute fruit evenly. Spoon into the dish and level the surface.

Bake in the oven for about 40 minutes until set and golden brown. Serve warm or cold, cut into slices; decorate with whipped cream, glacé cherries and angelica.

Serves 4.

PEAR & PASTA PUDDING

90 g (3 oz/⅔ cup) macaroni
500 ml (16 fl oz/2 cups) milk
2 pears
60 g (2 oz/⅓ cup) raisins
finely grated peel of 1 lemon
½ teaspoon ground cinnamon
3 teaspoons light soft brown sugar
1 egg, separated
30 g (1 oz/6 teaspoons) butter
bay leaf, to decorate

Preheat oven to 180C (350F/Gas 4). Grease an ovenproof dish. Put macaroni and milk into a saucepan. Bring to the boil, then simmer for 10 minutes. Remove from heat.

Peel and core one pear. Chop roughly and add to macaroni with raisins, lemon peel, cinnamon, sugar and egg yolk. In a bowl, whisk egg white until stiff. Gently fold into macaroni mixture, then pour into the dish. Bake in the oven for 30 minutes.

Peel and core remaining pear. Cut into slices lengthwise. Arrange decoratively on top of the pudding. In a saucepan, melt butter. Brush over pears. Return to the oven for 10 minutes until pear slices are brown. Serve, decorated with a bay leaf.

Serves 4.

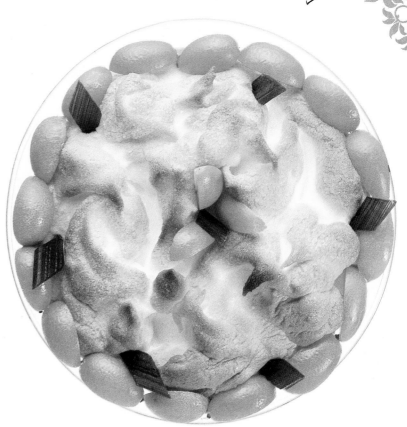

CHOCOLATE SPAGHETTI

MERINGUE PUDDING

60 g (2 oz) plain (dark) chocolate	
2 eggs	
220 g (7 oz/1¾ cups) strong plain flour	
chocolate flowers, to decorate	
WHITE CHOCOLATE SAUCE:	
60 g (2 oz) white chocolate	
155 ml (5 fl oz/⅔ cup) double (heavy) cream	

Melt chocolate in the top of a double boiler or a bowl set over a saucepan of simmering water. Make pasta, see page 51, adding melted chocolate to egg. Leave to rest for 30 minutes.

Roll out pasta. Roll pasta sheets through the spaghetti cutter. Put a tea towel over the back of a chair. Spread spaghetti out and leave to dry for 30 minutes. In a large saucepan of boiling water, cook spaghetti until tender. Drain.

Meanwhile, make sauce, put white chocolate and cream into a saucepan. Heat gently until melted, then stir until smooth. Drain spaghetti. Serve with sauce, decorated with chocolate flowers.

Serves 4.

125 g (4 oz/¾ cup) small pasta shapes	
440 ml (14 fl oz/1¾ cups) milk	
90 g (3 oz/⅓ cup) caster sugar	
finely grated peel of 1 orange	
2 eggs, separated	
30 g (1 oz/6 teaspoons) butter	
kumquat segments and angelica leaves, to decorate	

Put pasta shapes and milk into a saucepan. Bring to the boil, then simmer gently for 20 minutes, or until pasta is tender and milk has been absorbed, adding more milk if necessary. Meanwhile, preheat oven to 150C (300F/Gas 2).

Stir 30 g (1 oz/6 teaspoons) sugar into pasta, then stir in orange peel and egg yolks. In a small saucepan, melt butter. Add to pasta mixture. Pour into an ovenproof dish.

In a bowl, whisk egg whites until stiff. Whisk in all but 1 teaspoon of remaining sugar. Spoon or pipe over pasta mixture. Sprinkle with remaining sugar. Bake in the oven for 30 minutes, or until golden brown and crisp. Serve at once, decorated with kumquat segments and angelica leaves.

Serves 4.

INDEX